TRIBAL KNOWL
Practical Use of ISO, Lean and Six
Sigma Together

Copyright

Disclaimer and or legal notices

Published By Marnie Schmidt

Table Of Contents

Table of Contents

WHY READ THIS BOOK?

If you are looking for new ways to incorporate the popular tools of lean and Six Sigma with your traditional ISO9001 or quality system, this book is for you. Some people believe that "ISO is dead", and the field of quality is moving on to newer ideas. I say, some of the oldest quality principles as introduced by Juran, Deming, Crosby and Shewhart are still alive and well. In some cases, they've been renamed and repackaged, but the basic tools are still the same. They've been incorporated in the International ISO standards, lean, Six Sigma and most every other quality system in practice today. But, their effectiveness and simplicity is still as elegant as it ever was. Here is a good history of some of the legendary masters of quality:
http://www.businessballs.com/dtiresources/quality_management_gurus_theories.pdf

It's great to learn about the many principles of quality. But it's not enough to understand the theories. There has to be *effective application* of the theories to see significant improvement. This book is written in no-nonsense English for practitioners who aren't afraid of getting their hands dirty. This is a collection of real life stuff – tribal knowledge - about how to effectively use these versatile tools together to create remarkable performance in your organization.

I'm a big endorser of ISO9001, QS9000, AS9100, TS16949, ISO14001 and all of those broad sweeping industry quality standards because they are very well designed with input from international committees of subject matter experts. Unfortunately, they share the legacy of so many quality principles in that, regardless of how good they are in theory, they are rarely implemented effectively. That creates a stigma that the quality industry has been challenged with throughout its history.

Quality management systems have been around for decades, and have evolved quite a bit over time through their own commitment to continual improvement. However, there has always been an invisible barrier between operations and quality. When lean and Six Sigma were introduced as an alternative to traditional quality systems, operations and production folks took to them right away because, they prefer the hands-on nature and focus on improving productivity and cost. Many companies abandoned their ISO-based quality systems to try these new concepts of lean and Six Sigma. But lean and Six Sigma work best within a well-designed quality management system. Even further, the old *quality* management system concept has evolved into simply being called the "management system", because so many companies are incorporating their quality, safety, environmental and overall business practices into one central system. Companies taking this approach are seeing their "ISO" systems transformed into real, value-added systems. The whole concept of "ISO" initially was to provide a common business model standard that was effective and verifiable for certification by periodic, independent surveillance.

Somehow, over time, the "ISO" concept devolved in many companies into merely a pursuit of a certificate, but being disconnected from the real business, activity. So, as lean and Six Sigma entered the scene, they were embraced as a lifeboat to rescue companies from their failed "ISO" journey. But, in reality, lean and Six Sigma are most successfully implemented when there is an already established process-oriented framework and infrastructure of a solid management system. As lean and Six Sigma are implemented, they are introduced as defined processes within the quality system. So they needn't be a replacement, but rather complementary tools leveraged to revitalize and amp up an existing system.

WHY I LOVE QUALITY

I started my career in the Detroit automotive manufacturing industry. I have worked with many different quality management systems, including the supplier quality systems required by major automotive manufacturers prior to QS9000 (modeled after ISO9001) including General Motors' Targets for Excellence, Ford Q1 and Chrysler Pentastar. Working through the supply chain while at a metal stamping manufacturer, I had the opportunity to work with many manufacturing industries such as CNC machining, metal fasteners, heat treating, painting, plating, deburring, injection molding, blow molding, plastics extrusion, assembly and raw material supply including flat rolled coil steel, plastics and adhesives. And eventually, I became a part-owner of a flat rolled coil steel company.

I moved from Michigan to the Tampa Bay area in Florida in 2008. I became a Black Belt, and also began a whole new chapter in my life as an ambassador of quality. There's not much traditional manufacturing in my area, but I had the opportunity to join the exciting world of 3PL (Third Party Logistics), the transportation and warehousing of products like Gatorade®, Corona Beer®, bottled water and cigarettes. The logistics industry is very dynamic and its customers are fickle so they change their choice of warehouse providers frequently. This requires logistics providers to be very nimble and to be able to open a location and set up its systems quickly. As our customers required that all locations be registered to ISO9001, I used lean management to develop a quick start method to have new locations ready for ISO9001 certification within 8 weeks of startup. That was a very exciting time.

My most recent adventure was working with a battery recycling facility where automotive and industrial batteries are crushed and the materials – plastic, acid and lead – are reclaimed and recycled. This opportunity allowed me to learn much more about applying many quality tools and integrating three different management systems – quality, environmental and safety into a central management system with the intent to make the systems simple and portable. The company strategy was for growth by acquisition. With what I learned from the logistics industry, I developed a system that could be repeatable and quick to implement so we would be ready as the new facilities were acquired.

With each implementation, I took everything I had learned from the previous implementation, and tweaked it just a bit for the next one. My own story is one of continual improvement. And I'm not done learning! My passion is quality. I love to talk about it, debate about it, teach about it and share experiences with other quality professionals who have a true understanding of the importance and real relevance of quality and how it has the ability to transform a company and its processes from mundane to world class.

HOW TO GET THE MOST OUT OF THIS BOOK

It is assumed that the reader has a general understanding of the quality methodologies, "lean" and "Six Sigma", and general quality principles such as TQM total quality management, quality assurance and operations excellence. However, there are many useful resources throughout the book to help deepen the reader's understanding.

Throughout out this book, the term "OES" (Operations Excellence System) is used to describe quality management systems modeled after the International Standards ISO9001, ISO14001, AS9100C, QS9000, OHSAS18001, TS16949, and several other traditional quality management systems.

This book is intended to provide information about how to integrate all of these quality tools into a high performance, comprehensive business management program. Whether you are the CEO of your company or the person charged with leading the establishment of your company's management system, this book provides a number of real life lessons, examples and tips on how to use these tools effectively. I've included proven methods I've learned from working with a variety of different systems, with diverse company cultures in a huge array of industries. And I've also included several anecdotes which most every reader will either have experienced similar stories themselves or will be able to relate to.

INTRODUCTION

Traditional OES programs are often implemented with the sole purpose of obtaining certification to ISO9001, AS9100C, etc. When certification, rather than real improvement is the central theme, it is rarely successful. The implementation plan may include an overabundance of documentation, and a real disconnect between the system and the reality of the daily operations of the business. So much focus is put on the impending certification audit that something is lost in the process. And it is very typical for an organization to charge one or two individuals with implementing the system. They often do this independently, without the meaningful participation by *everyone* in the organization that is so critical to success. Ironically, the company doesn't ever realize the promise of improved quality or reduced cost, and therefore, management often views ISO certification or an OES as a "necessary evil" rather than a real path to improvement.

Lean manufacturing or lean management, however, is seen as a fresh idea for companies to achieve real improvement. Managers and operations folks believe in its focus on metrics, real life problem solving and cost reduction through the elimination of waste.

Many believe the two approaches, OES and lean and Six Sigma, are mutually exclusive. And companies who are forced to maintain certification to an ISO (or other) standard, due to customer or other requirements, are often frustrated. They can become less engaged in the system, and may establish a parallel group to pursue a lean initiative they feel might actually add value. Running an OES and lean in a non-integrated parallel is not a good idea, because it can create confusion about priorities. And it can send the message very clearly that the OES is only being maintained because it *has* to be. This can weaken the system, and at the same time, add baggage to your newly budding lean initiative. It's a better idea to integrate the two.

Lean management and Six Sigma can be integrated into an OES as complementary tools to absolutely optimize the resources used to produce your goods or services. All three have characteristics unique and critical to the effective management of a business. The first thing to understand about them is that none of them is a quality program alone, rather they are components of a comprehensive system.

A lot has been written about "management commitment" in the effective implementation of lean, Six Sigma and OES. But, commitment is more than believing in it and supporting a secondary champion of the cause. Top management must be the hands-on driver leading the charge to be effective. Especially at the initial implementation phase, they must deliver the message of commitment and engage daily in the process. Are there metrics to be defined? Management should participate. Are there deadlines to meet? Top management (not a task manager) should call for accountability. Are there deliverables required? Top management should drive the expectation. Are there successes to celebrate and lessons learned? Top management should deliver the message, demonstrating their hands-on commitment to the effort. One of the most common failures in implementation of any initiative is the failure of top management to *demonstrate* their commitment. Talk is cheap, but if top management shows the organization through their *actions* that it is important to them, it will be important to everyone else.

IN THE FIELD

One of my toughest cases was working with a company whose senior management team was highly invested in certification to ISO9001 and ISO14001, because their customer encouraged it. (It was later discovered that the customer did not require it, but they recognized it as a plus). *Unfortunately, the person who initially implemented the system did so with the sole purpose of becoming certified. He undertook the project as a personal challenge. He wrote lots of documents and created very complex systems for internal audits, corrective actions and management review, without input from the people who would be expected to use the system. He maintained the system with very little interaction with the rest of the company. People felt a real disdain for the quality program and really had no interest in participating in it. This was evident in the awkward interviews during their third party audits. Disengaged managers were put on the spot to feign their involvement in the quality program. It was also evident in the poor performance of the program overall. The management team was disconnected. Problems and nonconformances recurred with alarming frequency, because there was no effective corrective action program. And each time the third party audit happened, the company was issued major nonconformances to which the senior management was shocked and disappointed. This is because there was not a frequent interactive management review to review performance metrics and develop strategic responses. Further, there was no internal audit process at all, so the opportunity to routinely probe and self-evaluate for continual improvement opportunities was lost altogether.*

The saddest part of this story is that it is so very common among certified companies, but also because the program really did have a management team who considered themselves fully committed. Fully committed and fully engaged are two entirely different things. Companies who get it right have CEOs and Presidents getting into the mix. I've worked with companies whose CEO has taken charge of the entire system. They facilitate the third party audit process, report results and lead the effort to continually improve. Those are the companies who really get something out of being ISO certified. And they're also the ones, who welcome lean and Six Sigma and use them effectively. Their quality systems are the ones we call World Class.

What is the advantage of an OES?

ISO9001 and ISO14001 (and AS9100C, TS16949 and OHSAS18001 and all the rest for that matter), contain guidelines identified as critical to the effective operation of a business. They include the establishment of consistent policies that everyone in the organization is aware of and striving toward. There is a requirement that a company have critical items documented, and a process for controlling the distribution and communication of those documented requirements. There is a requirement that the key processes be identified, as well as the best way to do them, and a method is established to ensure this is done. The identification of key metrics so that the management can make good decisions is required, as is an effective corrective action process in the event the metrics or objectives aren't being met. And finally, a process to periodically check the effectiveness of processes and continually improve them is required. This is pretty common sense stuff and provides a framework from which lean and Six Sigma can do their best work.

The ISO model provides a great infrastructure, but only if it is constructed with lean and Six Sigma in mind. The design of the system should include the characteristics of being free of waste and excess variation. If it doesn't, this is a great place to start practicing with the tools of lean and Six Sigma. As a new OES is designed, it should done with a keen eye for waste and variation. The OES should always be simple and contain *only* what the company needs to be effective. This is where many companies get off track. With all the requirements in the ISO standards, there is a tendency to create a document or a work instruction for everything in the standard. This is unnecessary and what many managers dislike about having an OES. The OES should support *always* the needs of operations and their goal of making the company money. If the OES is designed with that in mind, it has a much greater chance of successful support by everyone.

Most companies who do have an existing OES have opportunities that provide terrific teachable moments lean and Six Sigma are introduced. Take a look at your OES and see if there is a particular area which people find cumbersome or bureaucratic. Ask whether a kaizen event could be used to pare down the process and make it easier to use. (A "kaizen" event is a small scope, short term project used to gain significant improvement in a process or area). If so, gather a team and do a very simple (and very visible) kaizen event that will be used to show your willingness to start right the OES for improvement. This can dispel the inevitable pangs of defensiveness area managers may have as they are notified that they will be participating in the launch of a new improvement program and their areas will be scrutinized for "opportunities".. Start with the OES as it is already. Identify internal customer complaints – what area managers don't like about the system? Acknowledge it, investigate it, solve it and improve it. This provides internal customer satisfaction as well as a terrific illustration of how simple a kaizen event can be, and how willing you are to use it in your own back yard as well as theirs!

Taking the opportunity to start out with a small kaizen event on your OES might also result in something unexpected. Fear of change is a common human problem. And so often, as I have investigated an internal customer complaint and proposed solutions, the actual complainants have a hard time following through to implement changes. They may be very able to articulate their dissatisfaction with a process or system, but resist changes when a solution is proposed. This is a weird human phenomenon, but it is very common. It is important to be aware of this phenomenon and have a strategy in mind to push through it. Change is tricky and does temporarily upset the balance of your systems. It is important to be selective in choosing what to change, and to be conservative in choosing how many things to change at once. If you can identify and implement a few carefully chosen changes and implement them effectively with support from most everyone on the team, you will begin to create a culture of change. This is a critical component of an effective OES.

How are lean, Six Sigma and an OES different?

Lean and Six Sigma are two methodologies used to sniff out and eliminate waste (lean) and variation (Six Sigma). Lean uses tools such as 5S and waste walks to identify waste. Six Sigma uses process sampling and statistical techniques to analyze processes and systematically reduce variation. The two share the powerful tools of PDCA (Plan, Do, Check, Act), DMAIC (Design, Measure, Analyze, Improve, Control), value stream mapping, visual management and a host of problem solving (root cause analysis) tools such as 8D, 5Y (5 Why?), Fishbone (Ishikawa), Poka Yoke, etc.

Lean is the most easily understood, and is often chosen as the inroad to implementation of a continual improvement program. Team members are taught to recognize waste and look for ways to eliminate it. The popular "5S" initiative is a high impact lean program that is very simple to implement. 5S is a 5-step program used to optimize a workspace – Sort, Shine, Set/Straighten, Standardize and Sustain, and it requires engagement of everyone involved in the area. The fifth "S" in the 5S philosophy, the "sustain" phase, is the most difficult, and as such, determines whether the 5S effort succeeds or fails. If the "sustain" phase is successful, it sets the stage for a high level of continued performance improvement through the implementation of more sophisticated lean and Six Sigma tools. 5S can be implemented in almost any work environment, because it is a simple exercise of making a "place for everything and everything in its place". And because 5S is used to create a workspace wherein only the items critical to the task at hand are kept and all else are removed, the concept can be applied in other areas as well. 5S can be used on *processes* such as design, engineering, purchasing and sales. It can be especially effective at removing unnecessary steps or forms in a process, if applied correctly.

NOTE: Companies using a fully integrated management system

including safety, environmental and quality often refer to this as "6S", as improved safety occurs as a natural result of 5S.

Using 5S is not limited to a physical workspace. For example, your sales team could use 5S to optimize the sales process. They could create a simple process map indicating the "touch points" with the customer, data entry, forms and paperwork. They could then trace back through the process map asking, "Is the customer willing to pay for this step?". They could then, potentially, remove any redundant steps, entries, papers, to optimize the process overall. This is a great team project, because each member of the team gets the opportunity to participate in the process. And the point of an exercise such as this one is to simplify the process, which pays off for the team in that they get the same result (or a better result) with less effort.

"Waste Walks" are also a very popular lean concept requiring teams to go directly to where the work is happening to look for waste. This idea helps foster an environment of interaction and empowerment of employees, and it helps to get the whole team on the same page of creating a war against waste in the business. Both 5S and waste walks are very hands-on and can be applied early on in the design and implementation of an OES.

Six Sigma is more sophisticated and uses statistical techniques to analyze data from a process, and provides methods for eliminating the sources of variation. As variation is a form of waste and a source of quality errors, it is very important to minimize variation in order to maximize efficiency and quality. Because the tools require more skill and education, it is common to create an organization of learners and practitioners (Black belts, Green belts, Yellow belts) with a hierarchy progression of demonstrated application. And there are a couple of key components you should create early, that will be used by your Six Sigma team later such as process maps, control plans and FMEAs.

How Do They All Work Together?

Lean and Six Sigma are techniques used to find and eliminate waste (lean) and variation (Six Sigma). They are process oriented and very hands-on. Engineering types love lean and Six Sigma. An OES, on the other hand, provides the higher level framework from which to use the lean and Six Sigma tools. And OES helps the organization identify itself – who is in charge, what the company does, how it's organized, how it works. This is critical for the organization to understand collectively their mission, objectives and core competencies, and many companies miss the point during implementation of an OES. Top management is usually happy to create a business plan for their own use, but leaves the "ISO or OES stuff" to a quality manager or management representative. Not understanding they are one and the same, the OES often becomes ancillary to the actual business. An OES is effectively a business model with some specific requirements to ensure the business plan is adequately detailed to help the company establish and maintain a consistent way of doing things. It then provides a method of improving as time progresses (and as tools such as lean and Six Sigma are deployed).

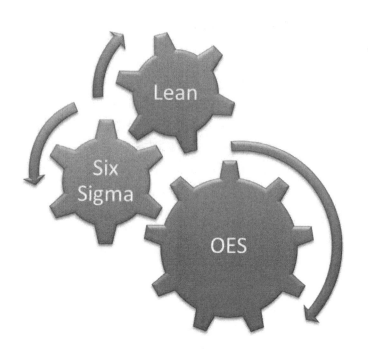

PREPARING FOR SUCCESS

If you are lucky enough to be setting out from scratch, you can seamlessly and simultaneously use an OES, lean and Six Sigma together to create a very high impact quality program. You should have a firm grasp of all three philosophies in order to integrate them effectively. So be sure to read, do research, attend workshops, obtain personal accreditations such as Yellow, Green or Black Belt or the many certifications offered by ASQ (The American Society for Quality) at www.asq.org. And join professional organizations to ensure you have a well-rounded pool of resources from which to pull.

It's fine to use the ISO standards as the overall pattern of your OES, but be very careful NOT to equate the term "ISO" with your new program. One of the worst things that can happen to your endeavor is for it to become synonymous with the term "ISO" and for "ISO" to penetrate the language your organization is using. ("We use this form because of ISO", "We had to document that for our "ISO" program", "ISO says we have to do that", "That's one of our ISO documents".). This immediately attaches the idea that the only reason it is done is to pursue a third party auditor's approval, rather than a deliberate, self-imposed discipline intended to improve your organization's performance. Avoid this at all costs, as it is very difficult to "undo" once the stigma takes hold.

The companies who achieve world class quality do it with a very well planned, fully resourced, deliberate strategy wherein *everyone* is engaged – not just involved or supportive – but actively engaged with real skin in the game. People (and teams, and departments and organizations) are motivated by self-interest. This is one of the most valuable things to be leveraged. Leaders of any quality movement must understand that people will participate if they understand how their efforts will directly pay off for them. And contrary to the sometimes negative reputations of

ISO, lean, Six Sigma, Total Quality Management as that "necessary evil", it's really not that difficult to convince people to get involved. That is *if* the builders of the system follow the right sequence and keep their eyes on the critical elements of an effective system, and if they are skilled at leveraging the available resources. Engaging the right leaders with the right tasks is very important. Done effectively, it can quickly deliver success to the team and solidify their commitment to the effort.

OES, lean and Six Sigma all address, each in their own way, the critical elements of an effective project as well as an effective process, so at each step, all three should be considered for applicability. If one can make the leap to understanding the connection in each of these areas, s/he can be transformed into a profoundly effective champion of quality.

EVALUATE YOUR RESOURCES AND COMPANY CULTURE

Before you start putting an implementation timeline together or arranging for your third party auditor to come for your compliance evaluation – STOP! Does your management team have the depth of understanding they will need to get this thing going? Do you? Are you able to develop and coach this team to the level of understanding they'll need? A competency gap analysis should be done. It is not enough for the "quality champion" alone to have the depth of expertise and understanding in all the disciplines you intend to employ – lean, Six Sigma, total quality management. It is important that the team make the investment in time to learn about the relevance and interaction of these methodologies, and more importantly, the ability to *apply* the tools effectively. Ask yourself:

-Does each member of the top management have at least a *broad* knowledge of the three concepts: lean, Six Sigma and total quality management?

-Does each member of the top management have a *depth* of knowledge in at least **one** of methodologies (lean, Six Sigma, total quality management) that s/he can use during the creation of the OES?

-Does each member of the top management have a realistic expectation and personal commitment to the implementation of an OES system *specifically* tailored to the needs of your organization? This means they intend to take ownership of the implementation of their specific area of responsibility not to stand behind the quality champion and cheer them on as they do it for them?

-Where there are gaps, are the members of top management willing to close those gaps prior to embarking on this implementation project?

-Has your top management agreed on the key components of an effective OES? Taking the time to get around a table and gain consensus on *each* element is very important. Does everyone agree on the importance of a formal training program? Does everyone support a document control system? Will everyone pledge to comply with ALL components of the system once they have been identified? Settling these debates prior to the creation of the OES will discourage resistance later.

-Is the company structure one of *process orientation* or are there still some silos or departmental barriers in place? It is critical to build bridges to create a process focus before this strategy can be successful. As you create a process model, there are many departments who will share responsibility for metrics. And there is no easier way to find resistance than for two departments to suddenly have to share responsibility for a reported metric, if they're not already used to this idea! This cultural hurdle must be overcome prior to proceeding. Your management team must understand and embrace the process philosophy to be most successful.

If your organization can enthusiastically answer "yes" to these questions, you're ready to go. If not, it's a transformative opportunity for your organization. You can begin a pre-infrastructural building project of creating a *process oriented* organization.

When a process focus has taken hold of your organization, you are well positioned to begin the exciting journey of establishing a high powered OES that will become the central functional hub of your company.

IN THE FIELD

Here's a doozy! I was hired to consult with a major mining company who described their needs as "We want to have Location A "lean" by the end of this year, and Locations B and C by the end of next year." We all know lean is a journey without a due date, but I looked past the initial statement to investigate further. After a couple of interviews, I learned that the company also had an "ISO9000 department". The management was very disappointed with the performance and return on their investment of ISO9000 certification, and I got the feeling it was because their implementation had been similar to the one I described earlier. There was a guy who did his thing in his office, and no one really understood what ISO9000 was, much less what they were expected to do with it. So the engineering manager decided to develop his own department called the "continuous improvement department" with the intent of implementing lean, and later Six Sigma. When I asked about the structure of the existing quality program, I was told that the new "CI department" was going to "do their own thing".

They went on to explain that the ISO department wasn't interested in lean and Six Sigma and they didn't want to be responsible for any new initiatives. And the CI department wasn't interested in the existing corrective action program and had no intention of working with it. They would snag whatever "real" problems came their way. After all, they were confident that the operations department would come to them for help, before they would go to the ISO group. Because the ISO corrective action program was just a hassle and a lot of paperwork, and they never really got any feedback on the reported problems.

Yikes! I spent several meetings working with a couple of internal bridge builders to try to confront and overcome this silo situation. Ultimately, they understood that under the current conditions, their lean initiative would likely end up like their ISO9000 program. They decided to take more time to work with the senior management to find a solution prior to moving forward with lean. This was a great decision, because your first swipe at implementing lean is your best chance. And creating the best environment to ensure your success is very important to the success of a program such as this.

Instead of giving up on a failed or underwhelming ISO program, lean and Six Sigma can be used to revitalize it, streamline it and make it sensible and useful to your organization. Let's get started!

"SAY WHAT YOU DO, AND DO WHAT YOU SAY" – BUT KEEP IT LEAN

There is so much emphasis (and misunderstanding) on documentation in the traditional creation of an OES. It is very common to over-document, and thereby lose peoples' engagement in the process right from the start. The only people who like paperwork are quality managers and quality auditors. It is critical to realize and *control* this as you create your OES.

Critical to your success is *simplicity*. Make your OES either *invisible*, meaning people are engaged and using it without even knowing it, or *irresistible*, meaning it is so easy to use that your team members cannot say it is unreasonable to expect their participation. Use lean and Six Sigma techniques like the identification and elimination of waste and variation to stop over-documenting before you even get started. Keep in mind, even if you're pursuing ISO certification, the standards do not require that you document everything – only those things that are critical to your business. Since your system is brand new, there is no reason to introduce waste or variation right from the onset. Do not write wasteful documents or duplicate documents, because duplicates introduce the risk of variation.

Decide what type of documentation (or combination) you're going to use. "Documents" may be anything from owner's manual-style narratives, to process flow charts to picture books to videos! Decide up front how your OES will cascade out. A good way to do this is to imagine you have to describe the system to a brand new employee. And just to keep some perspective, imagine that new employee to be a new CEO! A CEO will always want a brief, simple-to-understand overview. A traditional approach might be to present an official Level 1 Quality Manual, with an accompanying Level 2 Procedures Manual, with an accompanying Level 3 Work Instruction Manual, with an accompanying Level 4 Forms Manual, with an accompanying training process used to communicate the requirements and train employees. OR, you might have a simple OES or quality manual which states the policy, the list of processes you've identified (and how they interact), and who is responsible for each. You may then have a collection of process flow charts or videos (one for each process), and a list of forms used to manage evidence of the effective execution of your defined processes. It can be that simple. And remember, the CEO likes a 20,000 foot view. Keep it simple!

Process flow charts are a great way to go. And this can set the stage for a very lean documentation system. Process flow charts are perfectly acceptable as evidence (documents) to be reviewed during a compliance audit. In addition, they are a terrific precursor to lean and Six Sigma activities. Remember, lean and Six Sigma projects typically begin with an analysis of the process, sometimes using a process map or value stream map. Using a process map approach at the onset of your OES allows you to get multiple uses from the documents you choose to create. *Start* with a process map as the document, and it can serve as auditable evidence as well as the springboard for later continual improvement activities. And if you are very creative, you can even use the process maps as training documents!

As you begin to design your OES, resist the temptation to rush out and document everything you see happening on the shop floor or in the office or call center. Identify your external and internal customers first, then define the interaction of processes (and define which member of top management is responsible for each). You can begin to put together an initial timeline at this point, assigning the full definition of each process to the top manager responsible. Then, agree as a management team *how* each process should be defined and documented. Before these processes are defined, a *structure* and *method* for the documentation should be chosen. Creating a template is a perfect approach to ensure each manager is successful on their first attempt. The template should include input(s)-process-output(s), and symbols should be decided and defined on the template.

Your customer hierarchy and interaction of processes you identify as critical will become the basis for your OES documentation. As you begin to write, it's important to consider any regulatory or compliance items that *must* be included in your system. Your OES manual should be a description of your strategy to know your customers' requirements, your regulatory and compliance requirements, and how you intend to meet them as an organization – nothing more. That's simple enough. Where most companies have trouble is *after* the main OES manual is created, and the procedures or work instructions come in. It is very common to try to document each and every detail of each and every process. But, the main idea to consider is, how much detail is required to get from start to finish (customer product/service)? And at the same time consider, how much detail is needed to effectively communicate with the people responsible for doing the work?

Communicating expectations (customer, regulatory and corporate requirements) and the desired best practices to meet those expectations is the key to defining how much detail is required when documenting an OES. This means communicating expectations *within* the organization at the appropriate levels of responsibility with the appropriate level of detail to ensure people doing the work know what to do and how to do it. Does that sound a lot like training? That's because that's exactly what it is. A very common pitfall in the design of an OES is to miss the opportunity to incorporate the training process (including the documentation) fully into the system. Done properly, training documents can be designed to be an integral part of the documentation of the OES, as well as accomplish the task of training employees to achieve the desired goals of the company. Training documents can be used as "the" documents you'll present during an audit. Work instructions can be eliminated if training documents properly describe the processes.

DEFINE A DOCUMENT CONTROL PROCESS

So much has been written about document control, and so many different methodologies are available, that I won't spend much time on this topic. Ironically, though, with as much effort as is spent on creating and controlling documents, it remains one of the biggest challenges to maintaining an OES.

Everyone in the organization must understand the requirements and participate in the process. You must create simple and straightforward rules about the creation, publication and storage of documents. First, define what a "document" is and be sure everyone understands. You may make a statement like, "Anything that provides guidance on company policy, requirements or best methods must be controlled". This ensures that critical information undergo some sort of review prior to being communicated, and that references made available are kept current.

Beyond everyone *understanding* the document control process, they must also be able to use it easily. This is usually the tripwire for most document control systems. They are just too difficult for the user to use. Either, as a document creator, the process is too cumbersome to create and get approval for a document. OR, as the user, it is just too difficult to locate a document when it is needed. This is typically where the little notes and scraps of paper come from, where people create their own documents because they need them to do their work.

Be sure to consult the creators and users within your organization when creating documents. And for heaven sakes, keep your document system lean to make it as easy as possible to use. It's important that after the initial system is created, that people are willing and able to use the system to make changes. After all, continual improvement will most certainly create changes to processes as waste is eliminated and better practices are discovered. The key to implementing those improvements (changes) is your documented methods and a solid training process.

There is much discussion later in the book about using training documents to replace traditional written procedures and work instructions. One reason is the discussion we're having here. Changes are best implemented through training. If better methods are discovered, they should be incorporated into the training process to ensure *everyone* makes the process improvement together. Therefore, document control and change management are a crucial component of your OES as well as your training process itself.

IN THE FIELD

Documentation is a funny thing. It's commonly the silent killer of many quality initiatives. The documentation just gets so unmanageable that it eventually suffocates the system. Either the documents become unusable, or the lack of control of documents creates major nonconformances making maintaining certification difficult. I worked with a company once who had this very problem. Actually, they had two problems. One was too much documentation. And two was a silo condition between the training department and the operations support department driving the OES. The training department was unwilling to participate in the OES, and therefore created their own separate set of instructions to be used for training. They did not have a document control process for these documents, so they created a risk of nonconformance in their third party audits. The documents were also not readily available to the users. And the training documents, in many cases, did not match the controlled documents of the OES. Big mess. Further, the departments were not interested in working together to solve the problem. I ended up using a value-stream map scenario to help the senior management of the company understand the problem and work with the managers to work together. Eventually, the training documents were the only instructional documents in the company. They were created with the area managers' needs, they were controlled, they were available and they were maintained by the training department.

DEFINE A CHANGE MANAGEMENT PROCESS

Change is good, especially as it applies to the application of lean and Six Sigma. The whole point of kaizen ("change for the better" or "make good") is to improve. But improving for a day or two will not impact the business where it counts the most, at the bottom line. So, managing change is critical to the successful implementation of lean and Six Sigma.

Changes are very dependent upon people. If everyone makes a change together, the change can be evaluated, and further improvements can be made. If not, the change can yield mixed results and it may not be known whether the change was effective. This is why an effective change management process is so important.

The best place to start is of course, with documentation. Changes must often be reflected on part drawings/blueprints, bills of materials, work methods, operational controls, etc. Your system should include a simple change management process that requires all changes be reviewed for their impact on these areas, and require approval by the areas involved. It should facilitate notification to those who are required to implement the change, and to include the changes to the affected documentation. This will include document control at the engineering level (drawings), operations (control plan), and training. Other areas such as purchasing and sales are also almost certainly involved, but they often have controls in place for changes. They should be brought into a central system as well.

If your organization uses work instructions, but there are also training documents used for training, there is a very high risk of duplication and variation in your system. This goes against the lean and Six Sigma philosophy, and can also just create a mess. Using training documents as the *source* documents of your system whenever possible eliminates this hassle, and makes change management a lot easier.

Just like with any of the components of your system, the change management process must be easy to use or it may be circumvented. It is recommended that the teams responsible for the majority of improvements and change ultimately own this process. If engineering is most likely to launch and follow an improvement project, it is they who are the best candidates to be the "funnel and filter" through which changes are directed. Be sure to create something that allows a quick approval for simple or "like-for-like" changes. And be sure that, where more complex change management is required, it is treated as a process that flows nicely as an input to the normal engineering process. This will provide the best chance at success.

Having established a disciplined document and change control system, you are ready to start to create your lean OES.

BE *ALWAYS* CUSTOMER-CENTRIC

It is critical for businesses to know the customer, of course. The ISO standards contain a section *requiring* customer requirements to be identified. Lean and Six Sigma both require that inputs and outputs be identified in most of their tools. Inputs and outputs are much like a customer to a process, so they tie nicely.

Most anyone can get behind the idea that satisfying their customer is key to their continuing success, be it a business, a department, a team or an individual (whose most important customer is his boss). This segues back to why top management must actively lead the charge in an initiative of this type. Being a demanding customer of your direct reports, and clearly defining your expectations is essential to ensuring everyone is consistently working toward the same goal. Top management must follow this through the organization to ensure the customer needs are clearly identified and translated into internal customer needs within the organization. It's important to you if it's important to your boss, and your boss's boss, and his boss's boss, etc. If that chain is broken anywhere along the line, the initiative can fall apart.

So, this first step requires that all customer specifications and expectations are known. But, it also requires an identification of the hierarchy of customers, from the customer issuing the purchase order, to the board of directors, top management, department management, etc. There are many ways to do this, but a simple matrix or organization chart will do the trick. Few would argue that a clear understanding of customer specs is important and that they should be documented. So, this can become the first document in your OES system – and it's a useful document to boot!

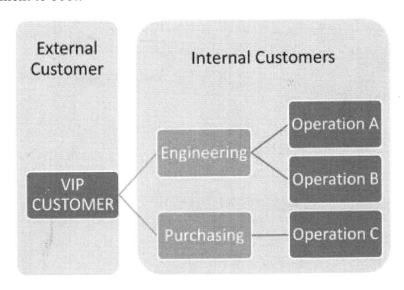

"Voice of the customer" also applies to lean and Six Sigma

projects. The "voice of the customer" should also always be at the center of any project. There should always be a measureable goal, and it should always be conspicuously identified as a customer need. Whether it's an external customer specification or requirement, or an internal customer need, such as an upstream process input or downstream process output goal, it should be identified as such. Keeping your eye on your customer will help you also stay on the path of minimizing waste. Anything that the customer isn't willing to pay for (or that is required by regulation or law), is considered waste and should not be introduced into a process.

IN THE FIELD

I once worked with a company whose customer was championing a lean initiative. The customer's directive was that their "supply chain will be lean by the end of the year". If you hear anyone utter those words as they begin to discuss a lean implementation, I urge you to get in the middle of that and try to redirect the energy into more achievable targets like a certain amount of training or a target number of kaizen events completed is a better goal than "being lean by X date". (A kaizen event is a small scope, short term project used for significant improvement). As our company had only one product, bottled water, we had only one place to look, our water packaging line.

A fellow black belt and I developed a terrific 3 day kaizen event model which included a full day of introductory lean and Six Sigma training, followed by a hands-on kaizen event. We gathered a team of about 10 people from the water packaging line including the area supervisor, line workers and material handlers. We also got the operations manager to sponsor the project, mostly because we wanted his blessing to proceed, but more importantly, we wanted him to validate the integrity of our data. As this was a pilot kaizen event at this company, we wanted to be sure we were successful. After just a couple of days, we had completely redesigned the work line. We removed bottlenecks, eliminated one line worker who was able to be reassigned to an area that was shorthanded, and eliminated a very cumbersome advance ship notice procedure.

The customer-directed procedure was for us to receive the case of water, remove the label, repackage the case to their specifications, and save the label. At the end of the day, the labels were scanned and sent in an email to the customer for traceability purposes. We were directed to save the labels. This was immediately identified by the line workers as the most wasteful point in the process. Saving the labels was difficult, because they were attached to shrink wrap and had to be carefully cut away. All the ragged edges of all the labels throughout the day made them difficult to stack at the shipping desk. And scanning them at the end of the day was a chore. A line worker suggested it might be easier to just snap a photo of the label with a smart phone, thus eliminating handling the labels altogether. The team was thrilled. At the end of the project, we ended up increasing productivity on that line by about 30%!

IDENTIFY THE PROCESSES NEEDED TO FULFILL CUSTOMERS' NEEDS

It is important when setting off on this journey to keep the scope of your OES to the business processes needed to fulfill customers' needs. Remember, anything outside that scope has the potential to be waste! The required business processes are likely to include receiving customer requirements (and orders), product/service planning (engineering), management of resources, procurement/purchasing/supplier management, product/service realization (prototype/sample/production approval), ongoing production validation/verification activities, training, internal audits (including manufacturing process & training audits), review of objectives/targets (key performance metrics), corrective & preventive actions and continuous improvement (which may include lean and Six Sigma).

You may want to begin with a common OES model such as one of the ISO standards. Follow the list of required processes, and perhaps use a flow chart to show the interaction of these processes. It is not necessary to include a great deal of detail at this point. Just a simple description of each process and how each of their inputs and outputs connect to each other will suffice. (Remember to gain the consensus of your team, and assign responsibility for each process to a member of top management). This process map can become the basis of your OES manual (should you choose to have one).

PLAN

RESOURCE MANAGEMENT
Provision of Resources,
Human Resources (Training),
Document & Data (& Record) Control,
Infrastructure,
Work Environment

ACT

MANAGEMENT
Commitment,
Customer Focus,
Quality Policy,
Planning,
Responsibility and Authority (org chart),
Management Review

DO

PRODUCT REALIZATION
Customer Process (Sales),
Quality Planning/Engineering,
Purchasing,
Identification & Traceability,
Operational Control,
Control of Monitoring & Measuring Equipn

CHECK

MEASUREMENT, ANALYSIS & IMPROVEMENT
Monitoring & Measuring
(Internal Audits & metrics),
Monitoring of Processes
(statistical techniques & data analysis),
Monitoring of Products
(inspection & testing),
Control of Nonconforming Product,
Analysis of Data,
Improvement (CAPA & Continuous Improvement).

39

TAKE IT ONE PROCESS AT A TIME

Now that you have the basic infrastructure of your OES designed, you're ready to start defining the processes. There are many approaches that may be taken, but again, it is imperative that the top managers responsible for each of the processes you've identified take personal responsibility for defining the process. The reason is commitment. The life cycle of a quality system can be much like fireworks. They start out with a boom and a big flash, and then begin to fade away. One way to maintain a manager's engagement is to allow them to define their process. After all, they own it. And if you want to maintain process consistency, meaning minimal variation and consistently following best practices, it is the manager who should determine what the process should look like. S/he should set the standard – no one else. It is wise for them to solicit feedback from their team, of course. But it is absolutely essential that they be actively engaged. Resist the temptation to push the project along by doing the work for them. You won't be doing anyone a favor, but rather setting the stage for resistance later. They may be relieved in the short term that they didn't have to do the task, but it makes it very easy for them to decide later they don't want to support the best practices, because they didn't define them in the first place.

Leading this effort can be the CEO, Operations or an OES leader, but again, it requires the absolute understanding and support of top management.

Start with a simple overview of ALL the processes, like the one shown above. Then perhaps choose a neutral process that the whole team is involved in – like performance review (or business planning, or monthly metrics review, whatever the preferred terminology within your business). Use a template and work together as a team to define what your performance review process should look like. Who is responsible? Who participates? What are the required inputs? What are the expected outputs? When is action required? What is the frequency of review? This exercise will help engage the management team. You will set boundaries together that you can all agree upon and hold each other accountable for. It is also great practice as each of the managers will set out to repeat the exercise on their *own* process(es).

Be sure to display the results of your performance review process map, and refer to it during your regular review meetings. Use it as a reminder to demonstrate, "This is what we identified, and this is what we're doing". And now it's time to assign a champion and due date to each process. You can use your initial process map to note who is responsible for each process. And have everyone commit to a date to review their process definition with the team.

A review of the processes is very important to allow the internal customers of each process to confirm their satisfaction that the interactions have been identified, as well as the appropriate inputs and outputs. There should be a direct tie between each of the processes. Each should be an input or output of the other, and should be able to roll up into the original overview process map.

For the administrative processes, a simple process map with responsibilities might suffice. The following is an example of a simple process map to further describe the process of Customer Process (Sales) listed in the "DO" phase above.

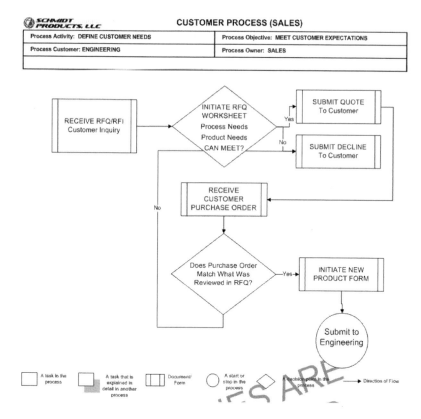

Where processes are more complex, such as manufacturing or transactional processes, more detail may be appropriate. An additional exercise may be needed to drill into the more complex processes. If so, it is beneficial to follow a methodical approach of looking at one department at a time.

DEPARTMENTAL 8 WEEK BOOT CAMP

From the beginning, most effort has been on simply defining the "who" and the "what". After the overall process map is known, it is time to start building the frame of the system. To incorporate lean and Six Sigma into a newly developing OES, a simple set of information (and documents) should be created. For *each* process, create the following:

-A process map (flow diagram) – describe the steps and include who is responsible for each

-A list of records required for the process – include regulatory docs, forms, etc

-An FMEA Failure Mode & Effects Analysis (optional)

-A control plan – include all critical control points including environmental, safety and quality

-A list of test equipment, calibration and measurement capabilities needed for the process

-Standard work for the leaders in the area – establish expectations and a daily routine

-A communication strategy – identify the expected topics, frequency and method

-A map of the workspace – identify emergency exits, major equipment, etc

-A 5S plan – include dates for implementation (by area)

-A list of metrics to be reported to indicate performance of the process

-A method of reporting the metrics within the department and upstream to management

-A collection of training materials – based on process map

-A training matrix – to ensure delivery of training and refresher training when there are changes

-A comprehensive audit plan – include the system, 5S, manufacturing best practices, records, etc

This is a big undertaking, but it provides the best chance for success in incorporating lean and Six Sigma into your OES. And once complete, provides that "irresistible" quality I spoke about earlier. Having these components in place creates a well stocked toolbox from which to work. And it's best to work through this list quickly. You'll start with the higher level processes of the OES, as shown in the graphic above. Then you'll move to a subset of Product Realization processes like "Production Control", which may contain several manufacturing or transactional processes used to create the product/process output your company actually sells.

One way to approach this, and one I've found to be consistently successful in the field, is to take it on in a project format. I like to use an "A3", a one page project summary to work through it. An A3 is simply a paper sized roughly 11 x 17, and it's a great lean way to communicate the goings on of your project in a simple to read format. I like to get the manager's commitment to work one hour each day for eight to ten weeks until the project is done. Each day, there is an expected deliverable. The catch is, the manager meets with me for the one hour, and I am responsible for delivering the output at the meeting the next day. This gives the manager an immediate sense of accomplishment, and helps to firm up their commitment to going on. They get to personally determine what is going in to the OES, so there's no reason for them to disagree or be reluctant to follow later. As the components are created, they are introduced into the department so that everyone is involved from the beginning. This is a great time to get input and engagement from the team. If you are coaching and leading this effort, it is very important to remember that in this scenario, the area manager is the customer of this project. These components of the OES should meet his/her department's needs.

I once used this strategy with an area manager, who was a retired member of the US Air Force who called it an "8 Week Boot Camp", and that name sort of stuck. He became very committed to the project, and was pleased with the results when it was finished. He continues to work with the OES as it was created, and actively makes suggestions to improve it. As the eight weeks wraps up, it's a great idea to invite the manager of the *next* area you'll tackle to tour the area you've just completed. Let the manager of the area proudly present their new accomplishments to their colleague to let them know what to expect when it's their turn. This promotes teamwork (and friendly competition), and helps to dispel some of the uncertainty a manager might have about participating in this process. Remember, you'll repeat this "8 Week Boot Camp" several times as you work through the higher level processes in your OES, and then onto the production/transaction processes used in "Product Realization". This methodology is a repetitive exercise which naturally becomes very repeatable. So it makes it ideal as a model to work through many departments, and eventually, many locations of a company. This method makes the OES fast to implement and very reliable, because it is lean, stable and easy to use.

In the next section, I'll stick with the "8 Week Boot Camp" theme and talk a little bit more about each of the components and why they are important.

PROJECT TEAM: J Flash, M Schmidt (Champion), J Doe, R Smith

PROJECT START DATE: 12-2-13

Describe the target (continuous improvement) project

Perform full review of process management systems and validate the process output

Current State

Process is not defined. Basic components of OES (Operations Excellence System) not existing or out of date

PROJECT TASKS

Date	Who	Objective
12/2/2013	J Flash, M Schmidt	Approve timeline and obtain commitment from senior manager and department manager
12/3/2013	M Schmidt	Send invitations to ensure action items are on team member's calendars
12/4/2013	J Flash, M Schmidt	Define the process (what/where) on process flow diagram
12/5/2013	J Flash, M Schmidt	Define responsibilities (by task or by position) - team flow
12/6/2013	J Flash, M Schmidt, J Doe	Define records to be kept - review hardcopy records, e-records, software versions
12/9/2013	J Flash, M Schmidt, J Doe, R S	Create an FMEA (optional depending on preference of the department and engineering)
12/10/2013	J Flash, M Schmidt, J Doe, R S	Identify control points (quality, safety & environmental checks) on a control plan
12/12/2013	J Flash, M Schmidt	Create standard work for manager
12/18/2013	J Flash, M Schmidt, R Smith	Standardize the environment by creating map of area with emergency equipment, exits, etc. Delive
12/20/2013	J Flash, M Schmidt	Define metrics - daily, weekly, monthly (metrics dashboard, trend chart and management review)
1/6/2013	J Flash, M Schmidt	Create training materials (based on process flow diagram and responsibilities team flow)
1/28/2013	J Flash, M Schmidt	Establish audit protocol for all control points and new standardized work area

PROJECT STATUS - TIMELINE CRITICAL

Week of	Status	Comments
12/2/2013	Met all objectives	All deliverables complete for the week
12/9/2013	Missed 1 objective	FMEA took 3 days to complete, but we continued with the remaining items for the week and they

DAY 1 – Meet with manager

Begin by obtaining a commitment from the manager by meeting with him/her and their direct manager (if there is one). Remember, it must be important to *their* boss to be important to them. This helps also to spread everyone's demonstrated commitment to the process. Show them the A3 and the tasks that will be accomplished during the 8 weeks. I find it helpful to start with a visual aid to describe the activities to be completed. Be flexible and let *them* choose the timeline. Do they prefer first thing in the morning? During their lunch hour? After normal business hours? This is a critical step in gaining their partnership. And let them choose the venue as well. It is preferable to work away from their personal workspace, to avoid distraction. But be sure they are in a comfortable place. Some people change their whole demeanor when they enter a conference room. Some people really don't like meetings and conference rooms, and this can create negative energy. If you sense your partner is uncomfortable in this type of space, change it to something more fitting to the manager's comfort.

As you discuss the timeline, explain that your commitment is to meet for no more than 59 minutes and 59 seconds, and stick firmly to that timeline throughout the project. You may encounter an opportunity to go a little longer during one of your meetings. Resist the temptation, and end the meeting promptly as scheduled. This does two things – it shows you respect their time, and it begins to set an example of the importance of time management and effective meetings (which will be discussed further later in the book).

Your expectation of each other is to stick to the task at hand each day during your hour long meeting. You will work together to get the required information on paper. And you will deliver a draft for review at

47

the beginning of the next meeting. This gives the manager a sense of accomplishment, and shows that their time is well spent. It also solidifies the importance of their input to the process.

This Day 1 meeting will seem very easy to the manager – all they had to do was agree to a daily meeting time and place.

PROCESS VALIDATION PLAN

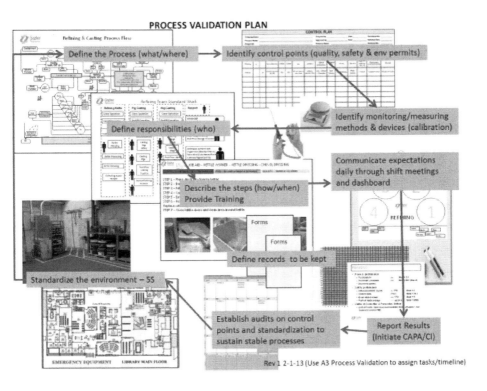

49

DAY 2 – Create a timeline.

Once you've committed to a schedule, it's important to get it on calendar. I like to use Microsoft Outlook to ensure these commitments appear on the manager's calendar. Create invitations for each day, and include the subject matter (as per the A3) to be covered each day. This will give them a reminder of the meeting as well as the content. Whenever possible, include templates that can help prepare them for the task of the day. This also allows you the opportunity to invite and solicit feedback from other subject matter experts as appropriate. In some cases, like the FMEA for example, will require input from many different people, and you can easily bring them into the process using the same meeting invitation. No fancy project management software needed here. Remember, lean means to use only what we need to get a job done. A meeting invitation works just fine for this.

Day 2 is pretty easy for the manager as well. S/he just has to accept a bunch of meeting invitations today. This sends the message, "this isn't so bad".

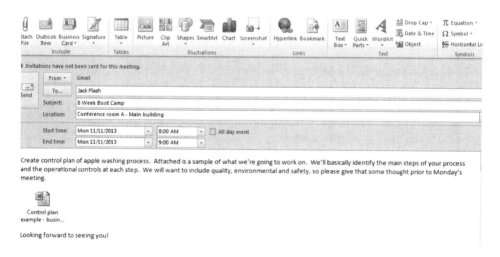

Create control plan of apple washing process. Attached is a sample of what we're going to work on. We'll basically identify the main steps of your process and the operational controls at each step. We will want to include quality, environmental and safety, so please give that some thought prior to Monday's meeting.

Control plan
example - busin...

Looking forward to seeing you!

DAY 3 – Create a process map (flow diagram)

A process map, as discussed earlier, provides a very easily understood visual description of a process. It is also a multipurpose tool which fits nicely into a lean or Six Sigma toolbox. It can be used as the baseline for a process map, which with additional data collection and analysis, can be built into a Value-Stream Map for Six Sigma to reduce variation and waste later.

Start by defining the boundaries (inputs and outputs) of the process. Then, describe the tasks in sequence to process the inputs into an output. It's important to have already defined a template and the symbols to be used to ensure you don't get bogged down discussing those details with the manager. Have an easily understood symbol key available, and get to it. You should be able to rough it out in one hour. Then, you will work immediately following your meeting with the manager to produce a draft document for the two of you to approve at your next meeting.

In one hour, you will have your first deliverable with the manager. This will show the manager a sense of accomplishment. Be sure to introduce and post the process map within the department. This will give others the chance to see the activity going on in the area, as well as give the opportunity for others to provide feedback to improve the process map if needed.

Having created your first document for the area, you have also created a very important document for compliance audit's sake. Auditors love process maps, because they are easy to follow. And bear in mind, process maps are much less likely to get you in "trouble" in audit, because they don't tend to include unnecessary detail that sometimes pops up in narrative documents such as procedures or work instructions. Keep it simple with a process map.

Be sure to deliver the completed draft of Day 3's process map on Day 4 – this will show the manager that you are committed to the timeline, and that you'll both be successful.

DAY 4 – Define responsibilities (by task or by position)

This can be done on the process map, or on a separate document. The reason this is created is to begin to define the structure of your training materials, as well as a tool to help your department manager or supervisor assign work. It's important to understand how work is assigned within the department to ensure the structure of the system matches what's actually happening on the ground.

For example, let's say a department making business cards has the following tasks – loading cardstock, printing, cutting, stacking, counting and packaging. Traditionally, there might be work instructions for those 6 tasks. But consider this. What if there are only 2 persons working the production line – one at the front (Operator A) and one at the back (Operator B)?

Operator A pulls up a work order on a computer, and loads the appropriate number of sheets of cardstock based on the bill of materials and instructions on the work order. S/he then loads the cardstock and hits "GO" on the line controls, and watches the printing and cutting stations for jams, misprints, etc. There are several safety items to monitor and lock-out-tag-out procedures should there be a jam.

Operator B is responsible for monitoring the stacker and counter and packaging the cards as per the work order. S/he is also responsible for cleaning up any scrap papers and making sure they are recycled as per the company environmental policy.

How should the work instructions be written? This is a very common obstacle in quality systems, and it is often because someone outside the work zone creates the documents. This is a great time to talk about work instructions versus training materials. When I stumbled upon the idea that training materials could replace and serve as work instructions within an OES, it changed my whole approach and was ultimately responsible for my beginning to incorporate lean and Six Sigma when designing quality systems. I had seen this disconnect with so many companies I had worked with, and when it finally clicked, I had a real "Eureka!" moment. I asked myself, "How much detail is required in my documented work instructions?" And then I asked myself, "What is the purpose of a work instruction? To satisfy an auditor? To show a person how to do the work? Both?" After probing this issue with several auditors, colleagues and peers, I decided the purpose of a work instruction was to define the desired method of performing a task and imparting enough knowledge to the people doing the work to perform the task successfully. To that end, I realized that these are effectively training materials, and should serve as such. Work instructions would be redundant, and I therefore eliminated them as part of my document structure.

Having said that, it becomes important as one is defining the process that the responsibilities for the process are mapped out as well. How is the work assigned? This should be noted on the process map, or a similar accompanying document, so that when training materials are created, they are appropriate to the work assignment. Consider the scenario above. Is it better for Operator A to have three separate documents (Load, Print, Cut) and Operator B (Stack, Count, Package) or one describing the full responsibility of their position (including the safety and environmental implications)? Remember, when there are "silos" within an organization, there are often additional documents, such as safety and environmental, that are written but not well communicated to the user. If these are treated as training materials, there is a much better chance that the documented procedures will be communicated to the users. Further, if the training department has comprehensive responsibility for ensuring best practices are known and followed, it is more likely that the documents will be user friendly and kept current.

Day 4 is used to simply consider and define who does what in the process. We aren't writing work instructions or training documents *yet*, but we are defining the structure for later. So, this day requires a lot of discussion and consideration, but ultimately, the responsibilities are simply defined by how the manager/supervisor assigns work. Operator A does this, Operator B does that, etc. This will become the plan you will follow to create training documents later.

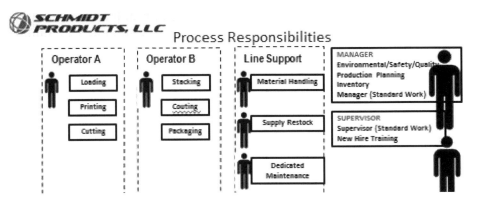

DAY 5 – Create a list of records

Of course, records are a major compliance issue. But often times, they are also an opportunity to reduce waste within a process. Are there too many forms? Are any of the duplications of information? Is there any redundant data entry? Once the required forms are determined, they should be monitored regularly through internal audits to ensure they remain in compliance. In the event that a lean or Six Sigma team comes into the area, this list should also be known so that they don't inadvertently "lean" up the process by eliminating a document that is actually required by law or the customer.

Your company should have a comprehensive list of *all* required records, and where they are maintained, how long they are retained, their method of destruction, etc. As you create this list for each department, the lists can be combined into one comprehensive list. This is a requirement whether you are maintaining compliance to an ISO standard or not – your local, state and federal regulations require records as well, so this is an important step.

DAY 6 – Create an FMEA Failure Mode & Effects Analysis (optional)

An FMEA is a great tool, because it can be created concurrently with a control plan. I say it is optional, because it may be slightly more than is needed directly at the onset of the OES. But, it is very useful when trying to prioritize areas of variation and risk *later* in the process. If your organization does not use FMEA regularly, it may be cumbersome to work with at first. If so, you may skip this step and focus instead on the simpler control plan. But I highly recommend FMEA as a useful tool.

Creating an FMEA will require more than just yourself and the area manager. It should include input from many subject matter experts and should most certainly include input from your environmental and safety experts to ensure it is comprehensive of the process. It could also, of course, take more than one 1-hour meeting depending on the complexity of the process and your organization's familiarity with the FMEA process. Be sure to use a template, and if possible, populate it based on the process map with the main steps of the process. This will get your team off on the right foot better than starting with a blank sheet of paper.

Process Function/ Requirements	Potential Failure Mode	Potential Effect(s) of Failure	S e v	C l a s s	Potential Cause(s)/ Mechanism(s) of Failure	O c c u r	Current Process Controls Prevention	Current Process Controls Detection	D e t e c	R P N	Recommended Action(s)	Responsibility & Target Completion Date	Action Results Actions Taken	S e v	O c c	D e t	R P N
ration 1 ate 11	a. Rust-slight	Some scrap loss	1		Storage or transit company	4		Visually inspect prior to accepting; checked again in subsequent operations	8	32	NONE						
	b. Rust-moderate	Excess scrap loss	3		Storage or transit company	2		Visually inspect prior to accepting; checked again in subsequent operations	8	48	NONE						
	c. Rust-severe	Can't use	7		Storage or transit company	1		Visually inspect prior to accepting; checked again in subsequent operations	8	56	NONE						
	f. Coil match	Wrong coil	3		Mill or transport company	1		Coil ID is checked against receiving documents	3	9	NONE						
	g. Gauge-(material thickness)O/S, U/S	Will not meet intended specification	3		Mill rolling process	4		D/OD readings are documented on computer inventory tag record	6	72	Obtain ultrasonic thickness tester to aid in detection of gauge variation at *each of master*	Guy in charge (by date)	Gauge rec'd. Receiving inspection updated to include expanded measurements	3	2	5	30

DAY 7 – Create a control plan

A control plan is critical for obvious reasons. It is a summary of the control points used to ensure the process is controlled and the customer's requirements are met. It is my favorite tool to also begin to incorporate *all* critical characteristics of your process so that your OES is comprehensive. Another pitfall of OES that focus solely on quality is that the affected personnel are charged with all aspects of their process including safety and environmental, and these are sometimes not included in typical quality-focused systems. To achieve that balance that all aspects are important, be sure to include them in your process control. A secondary reason to use control plans is because, if you are going to strive for certification to an outside standard like ISO9001, auditors *love* control plans. They are very straightforward and easy to audit. And having an auditor to give your control plan a onceover is a great idea, because they can point out opportunities that can help you make the most dynamite control plan you can have for your lean or Six Sigma team to work with later. An added bonus, is that control plans are very easy for *you* to use for internal auditing as well. You can include the control plan as the cornerstone of your process audit. Simply follow the control plan to confirm that the required controls are in place, they are being followed as defined, and there are records to confirm.

Creating your control plan is another activity that requires input from several subject matter experts within your organization. Be sure to include input from your environmental and safety teams to ensure all regulatory controls are identified. If your company has a testing lab, be sure to include the testing that is done in the process. Again, simply adding these experts to the meeting invitations will bring them into the process easily, and it will ensure the best control plan you can have.

CONTROL PLAN

☐ Prototype ☐ Pre-Launch ☑ Production	

Control Plan Number	Key Contact/Phone		Date (Orig.)	Date (Rev.)
123456	Mr Guy	XXX-XXX-XXXX	1/1/1999	11/12/2013

Part Number/Latest Change Level	Core Team	Customer Engineering Approval/Date (If Req'd.)
13	Bob, Sue, John, Jane	Favorite customer

Part Name/Description	Supplier/Plant Approval/Date	Customer Quality Approval/Date (If Req'd.)
Business cards		11/12/2013

Supplier/Plant	Supplier Code	Other Approval/Date (If Req'd.)	Other Approval/Date (If Req'd.)
NA	98765	NA	NA

PART/ PROCESS NUMBER	PROCESS NAME/ OPERATION DESCRIPTION	MACHINE, DEVICE, JIG, TOOLS, FOR MFG.	CHARACTERISTICS		SPECIAL CHAR. CLASS	METHODS					REACTION PLAN
			NO.	PRODUCT	PROCESS		PRODUCT/PROCESS SPECIFICATION/	EVALUATION/ MEASUREMENT	SAMPLE SIZE	SAMPLE FREQ.	CONTROL	

PART/ PROCESS NUMBER	PROCESS NAME	MACHINE	NO.	PRODUCT	PROCESS	SPECIAL CHAR. CLASS	PRODUCT/PROCESS SPECIFICATION	EVALUATION/ MEASUREMENT	SIZE	FREQ.	CONTROL	REACTION PLAN
57	Load	Feeder		Cardstock	Feeder		3mil	Micrometer	1	Ream	Digital mic	Reject to supplier
	Print	Printer		Ink	Print		100 x 200 resolution	Scanner	1	Each	Cont. Scanner	Stop printing; repair
	Cut	Cutter		Cards	Cutting		1 1/2 X 3" & square	Automated cutter	1	Each	Cont. Stacker	Stop cutting, replace blades
	Stack	Stacker		Cards	Stacking		Straight stacks	Automated stacker	1	Each	Cont. Stacker	Stop stacking, straighten and/or clear jam
	Count	Counter		Cards	Counting		500 +/1 1	Automated counter	1	Each	Cont. Counter	Calibrate counter
	Package	Box line		Cards	Packaging		500 cards inside box	Visual	1	Box	Final inspection	Repackage by hand

59

DAY 8 – Create a list of test equipment

Controlling calibration of your equipment is a critical process control. You should know what you have, how it should be maintained, and an adequate surveillance program to ensure your equipment is kept working properly at all times. This is obviously a high profile compliance issue for things like ISO9001, but also critical to effective execution of your process. If the monitoring plan fails, it can have catastrophic consequences on the quality of your output, or your ability to contain it should it fail to meet requirements.

Your control plan should be the main reference for creating this list. If your control plan is complete, all test equipment should be identified. As you make this list, be sure to update your control plan if something was forgotten. Be sure to include "between" calibration disciplines as well. If your frequency is six months, and an instrument fails calibration at its scheduled interval, everything it has measured since its last documented calibration is suspect. Be sure to have an interim quick check, preferably daily, to ensure you will detect a failure or trend should one begin to occur.

Maintaining calibration control can be done using software such as GageTrak. GageTrak is easy to set up and simple to use. www.cybermetrics.com/html/products/gagetrak/

But, it can also be done using other methods. Does your company already have a preventive maintenance program? You can modify that to suit your needs. Create scheduled PMs and make the instructions the required inspections and calibrations. This will track and keep records for you without an additional system being maintained. This is another example of keeping your system lean. Keep only what you need to get the job done.

DAY 9 Create "Standard Work" for the leaders in the area

Standard work is a staple of lean, but it has been around for a very long time. It has historical roots in early manufacturing and the military, and the concept is simple. Identifying and following a best method for everyone reduces variation and creates a stable work environment.

Consider the leaders of the area first, and help establish a routine for them to give them the best chance of success. What tasks do you think will ensure that work is assigned and areas are monitored to ensure the expectations of the shift, day or week will be met? You may have a manager, a supervisor and a lead, and they should each have their own unique standard work.

The manager's standard work may include verifying the supervisor has completed his/her standard work, but this should be limited. Focus on each individual's expectations. This can be documented and issued to each person to verify and turn in daily until a known routine is established. And it can then be used as part of your internal audit program. Verification that standard work, as defined by the manager, is being maintained and executed is critical to the ongoing stability of the process.

The standard work tool is also an excellent training opportunity. As new workers are introduced into the department, or team members are promoted, it provides a solid list of expectations from which to work. This ensures that the team member is doing what the manager expects them to do right from the onset. And the team member can be developed and coached using their standard work.

Creating standard work should take at least one day per position (manager, supervisor, lead), and should be introduced immediately upon approval. Get the standard work checklist out and in circulation. As the team members begin to use it, make revisions as appropriate according to their feedback. This will help establish the concept and your commitment to "best practices". It will likely provide you with ample opportunities to coach and team build within the department, as you begin to see that initially, not everyone does things the same way. But as you discover the differences, discuss it among the team and agree on a "one best method". This gives everyone an opportunity to participate.

	SUPERVISOR	1. Hard Hat									WORK LOG	
lame	S Nicks	2. Ear plugs										
lev	10	3. Steel Toed Safety Boots										
ffective	7/16/2013											
'ages	1/1/1900			7 am / pm to 7 am / pm							NAME	
tep	DESCRIPTION		1	2	3	4	5	6	7	COMMENTS/Corre
PRE SHIFT	COMMUNICATE WITH NEXT SHIFT SUPERVISOR									
	Accidents and NEAR MISSES in last 24 hours									
	Status of maintenance issues									
	Cartons printed and shipped last shift									
START UP	COMMUNICATE WITH SHIFT		Describe Shift Meeting Topics							
	Accidents and NEAR MISSES in last 24 hours									
	SAFETY TOPIC discussed (describe)									
	Kettles produced & yield from yesterday.									
	Changes or new processes? (describe)									
	Target to print and ship this shift									
During Shift	Monitor safe work practices - guards in place, lock out tag out available, PPE, printer ink labeled and stored									
	Assign housekeeping and small projects to shift workers									
	Monitor quality of printing, cutting and finished packaging.									

DAY 10 – Create a communication strategy

The most common denominator between every company I've worked with is challenges with communication. All companies struggle with this either internally, with their customers, with their suppliers or otherwise. It is important to get the group together and discuss what critical points should be covered, by what frequency and how to do it. Are there multiple shifts? Is there a shift startup meeting? Is there a weekly brief? Is safety discussed? Productivity? Quality? Create a solid day/time/duration and topic format. Use a bulletin board if necessary. This should be a highly visible activity. The area manager should be able to verify that this best practice is being done as defined, and part of the department's audit function should also include a confirmation of consistent execution of this activity.

This activity should not be cumbersome. It should be brief, but high impact. Create a clear and concise method, and make it "irresistible", meaning place it somewhere that doesn't require any additional effort by the team. For example, a time clock meeting at the start of a shift is a great idea. Everyone has to go past the time clock to punch in, so locate the meeting where everyone must already go. Provide a simple format with exactly what you want to have discussed. And have a confirmation that this is done. (I like to include it as part of the supervisor's standard work). Be sure the format includes important information such as productivity target for the day, safety issues, maintenance issues that might affect them today, etc. And be sure the message is consistent between shifts and groups.

Eventually, the goal is to have the team hold the supervisors accountable for this communication. Be sure to keep this a consistent expectation, and take the opportunity to take turns leading the meeting. This fosters participation and lets the group know this is an important new

63

activity and it is here to stay!

_____ Consecutive Days with NO Reported Accidents.		

Today's Safety Topic

Maintenance Issues
Work order   Issue
_____   _____
_____   _____
_____   _____
_____   _____

REGULATORY EMISSIONS
▨ ▨ (Check one) Meets 30-day rolling avg?

GOAL	Hour	Shift A	Shift B	Shift C	Comments
10/Hour	1	10	8	10	
100/Shift	2	8	7	11	
	3	9	5	12	
	4	12	0	11	Shift B down due to broken cutter
	5	11	10	10	
	6	10	11	7	Shift C down (LB went home sick)
	7	11	9	5	
	8	11	9	3	
	9	11	8	7	
	10	12	2	5	Shift B down due to broken cutter
TOTAL		105	69	81	

MESSAGES (Anyone may leave a message for the department)
_____
_____
_____

DAY 11 – Create a map of the workspace

This is important for compliance sake, but also as an important building block for 5S. The timing on this task depends on whether your organization has an engineering department who keeps these drawings current and accurate and readily available. If not, you may have to start from scratch and this can add time to the task. If you need resources to create such a map, college students studying CAD (computer aided design) can be hired on a limited term basis, usually at very reasonable prices.

It's a great idea to post the map highlighting the emergency exits, lock-out-tag-out materials, material labels, fire extinguishers, etc to let everyone know where things are. And this should be used as an audit document as well. Periodically verify that items are located where they should be. Report results back to the area manager so that adjustments can be made, where necessary.

Workspace maps are often used in lean and Six Sigma for spaghetti diagrams, workflow analysis, value-stream maps, etc. They're an essential tool in your toolbox, and a great starting point for 5S. Because, at the very least, the physical condition of the building and place of equipment should already be in place as you embark on a 5S initiative. A map of the area is a simple place to start.

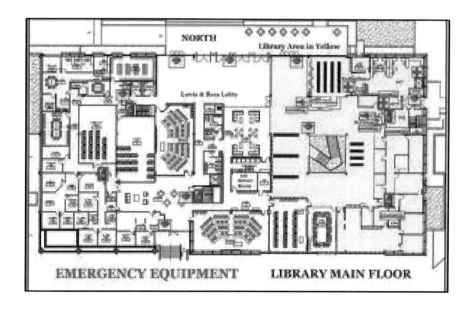

NORTH

Library Area in Yellow

Lewis & Ross Lobby

EMERGENCY EQUIPMENT   LIBRARY MAIN FLOOR

DAY 12 – Create a 5S plan

While you are organizing your thoughts in creating the OES, it's a great time to organize the work area as well. Beginning 5S can be a very visual demonstration of your commitment to installing a comprehensive OES, and putting some validity to it right from the very beginning.

A 5S champion should be assigned to, not necessarily complete a full 5S, but to put together and begin to execute a full 5S of the area. Divide the area into zones. You may want to have a "kaizen" event for each zone you've defined. A kaizen event is a short term, small scope project intended to produce a small, but significant improvement. Again, the A3 format is a great way to track progress and should be posted to show progress of the kaizen event.

For this part of the OES project, it is not necessary to actually tackle the 5S yet, but just to identify the areas and a timeline for implementation of 5S in each of the areas. This is typically at least 3 months in length, with additional months included for the "sustain" phase. This creates a preview for the area and affords the team the ability to get started right away.

If you'd like to start on 5S in the area, it is very easy to do. First, choose one of the identified areas and start an A3. Capture any particular areas of challenge including problems to be solved. Assign responsibilities and dates. Establish an audit protocol to monitor the "sustain" phase. The payoff here is obvious – 5S leads to improved quality and safety – that's a fact. But also, it boosts morale and makes a physical statement that quality and safety are paramount and will get the attention they deserve.

Implement 5S in the business card printing department.

Current State (Known Deficiencies)

Area is disorganized and tools are often lost - startup takes 15 minutes each shift.'
Hand tool expense exceeds $10,000 per month.
3 noted violations last environmental inspection due to unlabeled chemicals.

Action Item	Date	Resp	Action Item	Date	R
Divide workspace into 4 zones	2-Nov	S Nicks	Sort, set and shine zone 3	16-Nov	Nicks
Sort, set and shine zone 1	4-Nov	Nicks/Smith	Standardize zone 3 (est kanban rack for pkg mtls)	17-Nov	L
Standardize zone 1 (add shadow board for tools)	11-Nov	S Jones	Sort, set and shine zone 4	24-Nov	Nicks
Sort, set and shine zone 2	12-Nov	Nicks/Smith	Standardize zone 4 (chemical storage)	26-Nov	S
Standardize zone 2 (establish kanban rack for supplies)	14-Nov	L Bird	< Rack is backordered from supplier (due 20-Nov)	20-Nov	L

Problem Solving Team				Process / Training Team		
Problem	Action Item	Date	Resp	Action Item	Date	R
Chemicals are repeatedly found unlabeled	Design a process for labeling/storing chemicals	3-Dec	S Jones	Provide training on 5S to entire department		
				Provide training on kanban rack for supplies		
				Provide training on kanban rack for pkg mtls		

STATUS REPORTS

Date	Update
Week ending 2-Nov	Project started - zone 1 is production line and tool storage, zone 2 is supply area, zone 3 is pkg mtls area, zone 4 is chemical stor:
Week ending 9-Nov	Zone 1 is at 4S level - starting 5S level
Week ending 16-Nov	Zone 2 is in process - ordered kanban rack for supplies, but it is on back order
Week ending 23-Nov	Zone 3 is in process - need solution for chemical storage and labeling - formed Problem Solving team to address

DAY 13 – Create a list of metrics to be reported

Metrics are critical to process improvement, and critical to the business. They should *always* be customer-centric. Remember to only strive for what is necessary to meet the customers' (internal and external) needs. Expectations must be known or it is very difficult to achieve the goals established in the business plan. Like the process controls discussed above, the metrics should be comprehensive including productivity, safety and quality to ensure the overall output reflects all of the expectations of the process in the appropriate proportion. Productivity shouldn't trump safety or quality. A combination of all metrics should be expected to declare success. Compliance auditors will certainly review this information in order to draw a conclusion about the effectiveness of your system. And historical performance is also critical to benchmarking in lean and Six Sigma.

The best place to start is with the business plan. Regardless of the maturity of your OES, there is almost certainly a business plan with some basic profit and loss targets. Start there and identify which of the targets are affected by the particular department you're working on. Beyond the business plan, talk with the manager of the area. What are his/her goals? If the metrics are currently only defined to a monthly frequency, do the math and translate them into weekly and daily goals. This is critical to hands on operations personnel. Once per month feedback gives little opportunity to make critical adjustments to the process. Weekly, daily (and even hourly) feedback allows the team to know in real time if they're drifting off course. Then they can trouble shoot, and with additional real time feedback, they can know if their adjustment is effective.

Keep the number of metrics manageable, and be sure to gain everyone's buy-in on the integrity of the data source as well as the validity of the target(s). Ask yourself the following:

-Is this metric directly related to the customer?

-Is the data source reliable? Does everyone agree that the data is accurate?

-Is the target for the process coming into yours appropriate to meet your goals?

-Is your target sufficient to meet the needs of the next process?

DAY 14 – Create a method of reporting the metrics

Now that the metrics have been defined, it's very important to make the metrics known and visible. Metrics are almost always reported to top management, but surprisingly, they are often not reported within a department. A common complaint among workers is that they are aware they might not be meeting expectation, but by how much? Also, interdepartmental communication of metrics often occurs as an afterthought following a review by upper management. It is very difficult to respond to failed expectations weeks or months after the fact. So, it is critical to identify monthly, weekly, daily and even hourly metrics. Create a board and method of data collection and reporting, and assign responsibility. Takt time and other time metrics are a critical part of Value Stream Mapping, so this data serves many purposes in helping improve the process as lean and Six Sigma are deployed.

IN THE FIELD

One company I worked with did an extraordinary job of communicating performance. The departmental managers had a daily "standup meeting". There were strict rules about this meeting – it started and stopped on a precise schedule, tardiness resulted in a monetary fine, and any manager unable to attend was required to send a representative in their place to report their metrics and represent their department. The metrics reported in this meeting were posted on a centrally located board near the time clock. The metrics were for the day prior and were reported in color coded marker as meeting target "green" or not meeting target "red". It was a great management-at-a-glance aid to see which points of the process needed attention by the team, and it fostered a great deal of teamwork. As the organization's understanding matured, everyone understood that overall success depended on all processes being successful.

71

Each manager took the metrics from their own department and incorporated them into their own department's shift meetings and a metrics dashboard posted in their own department. Some broke down the data to "yesterday's finish" as well as a real time report by hour of the current day. This empowered each member of the team to see and respond to their department's current performance. Upon implementation of these metrics boards, the company saw significant (and almost immediate) improvement.

The daily metrics should also be translated into monthly performance for purpose of management review. The current month as well as previous months should be reported to show trends. Remember to design your metrics and reporting frequency to meet the audience. People with their hands on the process want hourly feedback, while senior management wants the "bottom line". The lesson to be learned is to keep the metrics aligned, so that they are consistent and the data is coming from the same source. The level of detail is changed to meet the needs of the audience.

DAY 15 (Week 3) – Create a collection of training materials

This is a very controversial area of discussion, and one of those areas where you might find your organization still has silos. It is common for the human resources department to be responsible for training, and about half the time, the training department understands their potential role in the OES and they are excited about it. The other half of the time, the human resources or training department wants nothing to do with the OES and that can be challenging. This must be worked through with clearly defined responsibilities and buy in from everyone. Decide who will own and maintain the training materials once they are created. And it is critical that the area manager be the *customer* on this. Training departments often work in a support role to operations. But they often create and deliver training based on their observation of the process, rather than a customer-driven definition of the desired methods and best practices. Participation by the manager ensures the training will be embraced and reinforced within the department. Sometimes, the training department introduces a method during orientation, and then when the employee is released into the daily operation, they learn the "real" way it's done. This is a toxic environment which makes the training department ineffectual and the operations department disappointed in the product they receive from the training department.

Bringing the training materials into the process gives both sides legitimacy and consistency. There is no reason to have an additional set of documents specific to the OES. Only create what you will use. Remember, what needs to be documented (and the level of detail required) is whatever is necessary to communicate who/what/how/when/why to do something in order to meet the customers' requirements – nothing more. When the training materials are created this way, they become live and relevant. They are used regularly, and where process changes are to be made, the documents will surely be kept up to date. This ensures good document control, as well as up-to-date training.

Training documents should be simple, and they should include all the information an employee needs to know in order to do the job to meet all requirements. This includes integration of safety, environmental and quality as well. Why should there be multiple procedures for the same task? Put all the requirements on the instructions for the task, and the employee will have the best chance for success. Also, as improvements are identified by cross functional departments, everyone will know there is only one place where the new methods need to be included – and that is the one training document for the task.

Start by going back to your original process map and assignment of responsibilities. How is the work assigned? If it is by position on the work line, write the training document accordingly. If it is by task, write it that way. Consider the start of shift – when the supervisor points to someone and assigns a task, that person should be able to go to one document to remind them the key points of their work.

Training documents should not be expected to substitute for good training. Human interaction, formal instruction, apprenticeship should still be an integral part of the training process. The training documents should simply serve to facilitate the training process (and reinforce it as a reference, when necessary).

Training documents should be very visual in nature, and should include photos or graphics whenever possible. There are so many reasons for this, among them ease of understanding, overcoming language barriers, providing simplicity, and overcoming communication challenges (such as a noisy work environment, a respirator required environment, etc). Posting training documents at point of use is also highly recommended. It prevents the user from having to search for the document, and it provides the opportunity to coach and reinforce best practices. If it is observed that a team member is not performing a task as identified as a best practice, they can be coached on the spot using a visual reminder of the established method.

I like to use a color coded job aid with lots of photos. I like to include *all* aspects of the job including safety, environmental and quality. Are special safety practices required? Are special disposal or labeling requirements a part of the process? What quality indicators are important? Include photos of poor safety, nonconforming conditions of the area, and photos of nonconforming product where applicable.

The amount of time required to create this collection of training documents varies depending on the number of steps, photos required and input from subject matter experts needed. I like to meet with the manager and define the steps, then take photos to highlight the important items in each step. I always target completing one training document per day during this time period, but sometimes one task can be particularly complicated and may take more than one day. To ensure you stay on track, make a list of the training documents needed and estimate a time for each. Update your meeting invitations to reflect your plan.

IN THE FIELD

Training documents needn't be complicated. I once worked with a very small "mom & pop shop" manufacturer, as we called them in Detroit. Because they were an automotive parts supplier, they too were required to be ISO9001 (actually QS9000) registered to be an approved supplier to the Big 3 automotive companies. The owner there was also the company's quality manager, and she was a sprite! She was lean before lean was cool! She really embraced the idea of "nothing but what is absolutely necessary". Her documented training program included a blueprint stuck to the wall with a large piece of butcher paper, with the drawing number and revision level hung below it. When she trained a new employee on the one simple assembly process her company performed – insert grommet into widget – she had the employee sign and date the butcher paper. Training needs? This drawing. Training document? This blueprint. Training evidence? This signature and date. Her third party auditor inquired with several of her assembly workers and they were all able to demonstrate their competency. She passed her audit with flying colors! No nonconformances. Not even any "opportunities for improvement". She inspired me.

DAY 35 (Week 6) – Create a training matrix

This is the simplest form of a plan, visual manager and training record all in one. It can show at a glance, what training is needed, who is trained, and who needs training. When changes occur, it can give a quick glance of who should be retrained. And if you include dates, it can tell you who should have refresher training to ensure the methods are still the same and they are still being followed. As your best practices are identified, it is critical that the training documents are updated and refresher training is given. Also, an audit protocol should be established to verify that the changes have been made and everyone is following the changed process consistently. Verification of effectiveness (or an ongoing audit) of training is critical to creating stable processes and a competent work team.

The training department should begin delivering the new training immediately. Record who has been trained to the new methods. And differentiate between demonstrated competency and proficiency sufficient to warrant training of others. Again, this gives the team a sense of accomplishment. As the matrix is populated, the manager and supervisor get the deliverable product of good training from the training department. And the employees being trained begin to see their skills inventories build. As personnel/resource requirements change, it's also a terrific way to quickly understand who has demonstrated competency in a skill should they be called upon to perform it or cover for another team member.

TRAINING MATRIX

SCHMIDT PRODUCTS, LLC — Rev 2 7-11-3.

	30 Days					60 Days			90 Days	
	Housekeeping	5S	Loading Feeder/Cutter	Lockout/Tagout Feeder/Cutter	PM Feeder/Cutter	Operating Stacker/Pkg Line	Lockout/Tagout Stacker/Pkg Line	PM Stacker/Pkg Line	Oversee Line Operation	
Revision	1	1	1	2	1	3	1	1	1	1
Smith, Jane	Jan-99	Jan-99	Jan-99	Jan-99	Jan-99	Oct-13	Feb-99	Feb-99	Mar-99	Mar
Doe, John	Jul-12	Jul-12	Jul-12	Jul-12	Jul-12		Aug-12	Aug-12	Sep-12	Sep
Public, John Q	Aug-06	Aug-06	Aug-06	Aug-06	Aug-06		Sep-06	Sep-06	Oct-06	Oct
Jones, Susan	Mar-09	Mar-09	Mar-09	Mar-09	Mar-09	Oct-13	Apr-09	Apr-09	May-09	May
White, Robert	Dec-12	Dec-12	Dec-12	Dec-12	Dec-12	Oct-13	Jan-13	Jan-13	Feb-13	Feb

Legend
Requires training (or refresher/change to process)
Demonstrated proficiency - can perform the task alone
Highly proficient - authorized to train others

DAY 40 (Week 7) – Create an audit plan for the area

Without an audit plan, you will likely not sustain all the standards you have worked so hard to create. As a process is defined, training must be provided to ensure the best practices will be carried out. The best way to ensure they are carried out is through surveillance. A robust audit protocol will give the department frequent and data-driven feedback about how well they are meeting their commitment. If things start to slide, the area manager and his team can be made aware of it quickly so that it may be corrected. An audit portfolio might include:

-Control plan – verify the control points, records and calibration of equipment

-Manager, supervisor, lead standard work – verify the standard work is being done consistently

-Communication – verify the established meeting plan is being followed and is effective

-Area map – confirm location of emergency equipment, exits, fire extinguishers

-5S – create a 5S audit with specific conditions and scoring to ensure 5S is sustained

-Training – verify (on a rotating basis) all established documented best methods (training)

-Training – spot check the training matrix – all trained? Any changes? Training given?

-Summary of audit results for the area

Set up a matrix and audit protocol for these items – who will audit, how often, how to report findings? Be sure the audit protocol includes easily reported results and trends, so that improvement can be shown as it happens. This is very important because initially, it is likely that the audits will reveal several opportunities and gaps during implementation. You want the area manager to see improvement right away so that they don't lose enthusiasm. Make the audit report clear and easy to identify improvement.

DAY 45 (Week 8) – Take a bow!

Week 8 should be spent reviewing what you've spent the past 7 weeks building. Hopefully, you've created a visual workspace starting with your project overview graphic and A3. As you progressed through the weeks, you should have added your accomplishments to this display. This creates a very real visual reminder of the progress you've made and the system as it is being built.

At the end of the eight weeks, invite representatives of your next "8 Week Boot Camp" target to come to the area you've just finished. Let the area manager present their process flow, control plan, training materials and communication process, and have them host a tour of the area showing their progress with 5S. This provides a great opportunity to congratulate the team for having finished their boot camp, while welcoming the next team into the process. They can see exactly what is expected, and they can see that a colleague has successfully completed the journey they are about to begin.

I've used this method several times and it really helps to make the experience one to look forward to, rather than that old "necessary evil". The department managers begin to mentor one another. Each one, having the opportunity to see their peers' success, wants to meet the expectations and then "one up" their counterparts. It's a great motivator and does wonders to promote the ongoing philosophy of continual improvement, which is so important to your ongoing success.

IMPLEMENT A COMPANY WIDE INTERNAL AUDIT PROGRAM

Once you have completed the "8 Week Boot Camp" on each process, and have finished with an audit protocol for each, a comprehensive audit plan should be established. Internal audits are one of the most powerful (and most underutilized) of all the quality tools.

With our friends at the IRS, the term "audit" generates negative feelings right from the onset. Regardless of the unpleasant term, audits are your friend. They are absolutely necessary to ensure a newly implemented process or method becomes stable. Consider the adage, "It takes 28 days to make a habit". New processes and methods are simply habits we need to develop. And they don't happen without consistent oversight until they do become habit.

Internal audits are also a requirement of the ISO standards, so if you're going to maintain certification, you are required to have an audit plan. As long as it's required, you might as well make yours outstanding and effective. Keep it lean. If it doesn't serve your organization, it's waste!

First, create an internal audit team. Solicit the company for a good representative sample of people at many levels of the company. If you're certified to one of the ISO standards, your registrar probably has internal auditor training available. And there are countless companies in the general quality market who provide this training both remotely and on your site. ASQ (American Society for Quality) has a good Certified Quality Auditor program. www.asq.org. But, keeping it lean, I like to conduct internal audit workshops to train internal auditors.

I structure the workshops so that basic auditing skills are taught, and the specific company's audit policy and procedure are followed. Following that, we use the company's audit plan and pick a couple of audits that are due. We actually conduct the audits that are due as a real life exercise. This is a very popular option among hands-on types. There are certainly people within your organization who might be very open to participating in the internal audit process, but just don't have the patience to attend classes on quality theory. They like to dig right in and get to work. Harness this energy by creating a workshop that ends with a finished audit or two. You'll be glad you did. The auditors in training are afforded the benefit of your guiding hand as they work through the audit process. If they have any trepidation about whether they can perform an audit, it will quickly dispel with you standing by all the way. You will be auditing actual processes or areas within the company that are germane to their experience and skills. They will understand what they're looking at, and will begin very quickly to know how to dig for answers. As they become engaged in the process, they will also have a much greater understanding of the audit process and that it should not be intimidating. They will welcome an audit when it comes to their turn to be the auditee.

Once the workshop is complete, each auditor in training should be paired with a qualified Lead Auditor to apprentice with until they are qualified to lead an audit on their own. Each auditor is unique and may require more or less training and practice. I target, say, 5 audits minimum before the auditor in training can be evaluated for Lead Auditor status. It takes practice to become a truly effective auditor. Be sure your training program provides the opportunity to learn and practice, practice, practice!

Create a disciplined training process which clearly defines what training is needed, and what is necessary to demonstrate competency. Perhaps the Lead Auditor should provide an evaluation for each of the apprentice's audits until they reach a defined level of ability? This can be done with a simple survey to be completed by the Lead Auditor. Or you may choose to use a Lead Auditor panel to discuss each apprentice auditor's skill level, based on their experience conducting audits with them. Whatever you choose, be sure to define it upfront so the person in training understands their progress every step of the way.

As your internal audit team begins to gel, be sure to plan each audit event pairing the most appropriate auditors to the area to be audited. Of course, no auditor should ever audit their own work. This negates objectivity. But there is value to carefully selecting the "right" auditor for the job. Understand your auditors' work history, areas of expertise and interests. The operations guy may be particularly interested in the purchasing process, because he is the customer of that process, and may have valuable insight. Be careful, though, not to select an auditor is this scenario who might be predisposed to criticizing an area based on his customer experience. Choose the auditor who can be most objective, but also someone who can understand the process quickly and thereby provide a good review and observations.

I've found a simple way to manage internal audit plans. As shown above in the process specific audit plan, there should be a company-wide audit plan summarizing the performance in each of those areas. Create a company-wide matrix and audit report and be sure to include:

-Systems audits – audit the highest level processes against your applicable ISO standards

-Process audits – pick an audit of a department's control plan audit and summarize

-Standard work – create a reporting method to summarize all departmental standard work audits

-Communication – create a reporting method to summarize communication performance

-5S – create a reporting method to summarize 5S scores (by department)

-Training – create a reporting method to summarize matrix performance

Consider using Outlook to manage and schedule your audits. Again, rather than introduce an additional software program, use what you already have and what is familiar to your organization. I use meeting invitations to schedule audits. I like to include the audit form (depending on what is to be audited), and a scheduled date, time and place. This makes the effort easier for each member of the audit team, and it is also very easy to manage visually. Using color coding can show audits due versus complete, and summary of all audit activities can be printed out for review.

By sending a simple invitation, you can assign an auditor and invite the auditee(s). The audit form will appear in the invitation, so everyone can prepare for the event. The questions to be asked are known. Also, it is helpful to include the "last audit results" on the audit form including the last date, results and who was involved. So the previous audit results can be followed up on in the new audit. The invitation can also include the place and time, so it easily appears on everyone's calendar.

When it's time for the audit, the team will get a reminder and they just have to show up! The audit results can be recorded right on the appointment, so the audit record is created and filed in one easy step. This makes the audit process really simple on the team's part. Less effort means you'll be more likely to get participation. Making it irresistible is the name of the game.

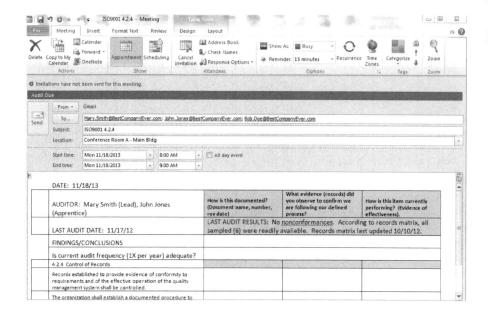

IN THE FIELD

Very early in my career as a quality professional, I learned just how uncomfortable the idea of an "audit" can make some people. I had just developed a nifty new supply chain management process for the metal stamping company I was working with. And it was time to launch our "supplier audit' campaign. I made calls and letters to arrange these audits and sent the audit form to the suppliers to let them know what I'd be looking at. The audit form was patterned after what General Motors called their "Targets for Excellence" program which included all facets of operations, (not just quality). This program was very far reaching and quite involved. Because my audit form was just like GM's, it too was quite involved.

I arrived at one supplier's facility where I was cheerfully greeted by their salesperson. We had coffee and things were off to a very good start. I was given a tour of the plant, and then I was introduced to the "quality manager". I was not aware at the time, but the "quality manager" was actually one of the founders of the company, and he had been around the tough Detroit automotive business for a very long time. While I was just discovering quality management, he had been running his business for more than a decade. I began my interrogation immediately, and before giving him a chance to warn me that he was not a fan of this whole audit idea, I requested records and documents right away. He looked me straight in the eye and said, "You're so full of ......", and the audit was over right then and there. The salesperson was mortified, and it was an interesting audit report to say the very least.

Had I taken the time to talk with the quality manager and understand that he was very knowledgeable, I could have gained a much greater understanding of his business, which is, after all why I was there. My supplier management system had been created for the sole purpose of assuring a high quality stream of products and services coming in to my company. I really blew it on that one. I was a Certified Quality Auditor at the time, but clearly, knowledge without practice and application is little more than a nice idea. I learned from that experience and changed my strategy right away. In every audit since, I've done a lot less questioning and a lot more listening. I find the answers seem to come naturally that way. And I save my questions until the very end of the event. If something I need hasn't revealed itself, I'll ask then. This allows the auditee to present their knowledge of the process, and they really end up auditing themselves in the process.

There's a very happy ending to this story. I went to work for that company a year later, and that quality manager become a great mentor to me!

ESTABLISH A CORRECTIVE AND PREVENTIVE ACTION PROCESS

First of all, what is the difference between corrective and preventive action? Well, it's obvious that if we suspect a problem will happen and take steps to prevent it, that's preventive action. And if the problem has already happened, it's corrective action. But there is also a subtle nuance that is often overlooked, and that is the idea that if you solve or *correct* a problem whose root cause(s) could affect similar processes, you move into the similar processes and take action to *prevent* the problems from occurring there as well.

A wise mentor of mine once said, "The problem with problem solving is that we rarely solve the real problem". That's an idea that has really stuck with me. The critical part of problem solving is to correctly and *completely* define the problem. This is particularly true when working with customer complaints. It is difficult, but necessary to define the problem and support that problem statement with data. If you can't confirm the problem with data, you probably can't solve the problem. Because how will you know you solved it if there's no data to tell you so?

There are many problem solving methods, 8D, 5Y (Why), DMAIC, PDCA, Fishbone (Ishikawa), etc. But each of those methods relies on a clearly defined and proven problem. Otherwise, the next steps are ineffective at solving the real problem.

Start by confirming the problem with a sample, a photo, lab results, etc. And quantify the problem. How much of the lot is affected? How often does this particular problem occur? When does it occur – is it seasonal? Shift related? Does the problem happen to other customers (as applicable)? If not, what is unique about the customer's process that gives them problems that no one else seems to have? If it is an internal problem, does it occur only in one process or plant wide?

Once you have a clearly defined and proven problem, assemble a team or consult with subject matter experts to investigate how and why the problem happened. The 5Y (Why) method is my favorite, because it is simple. As a lean practitioner, I always try to use only the tools that I need. And 5Y usually fits the bill. Of course, there are other, more complex methods which I also use in conjunction. After all, the 5Y method might help me identify the root cause, or why the problem happened. But it may not tell me how to *fix* the problem, though I know why it occurred. Using people who use the process is typically the most successful approach to solving a problem. This is because they will have a wealth of knowledge about what has been tried in the past, and they will understand the interaction of their process with other processes. And this is important, because you don't want to solve a problem in one area while inadvertently creating a problem in another area, because you didn't fully understand the processes up and downstream. Solicit input from a good cross-section of users of the process to ensure that a proposed solution is agreeable and will be supported by all. Making a change to a process to fix a problem only works if *everyone* makes the change. Changing a process should always begin with training and be monitored using internal audits to ensure everyone has made the change and the change was effective. Even if it's a minor modification to an automated process that probably won't be noticed, be sure to include the users in the change. This creates trust and confidence in the team, and assures the group that their input is respected.

A culture of trust is important to the success of an organization. Admitting to having a problem is sometimes counter to our human egos. Publically having a problem can be very disconcerting. We can feel vulnerable and exposed. This is just part of our human nature. So, we tend to bury our problems or pretend they aren't there, rather than face them head on. If an organization can establish a culture of problem solving as inspiring and challenging, it can leverage that to do great things. When people are willing to recognize a problem as an opportunity to make change for the better, that is a powerful tool. So take time to dispel the myth within your organization that problems should only result in accountability or blame. Or that having a problem shows a department, group or individual's weakness or incompetence. Problems happen. It's what we do with them that counts.

IN THE FIELD

I once worked with a major US steel mill that had developed a proprietary product, which made them very profitable. This particular type of steel was made very thin and lightweight, but very strong by a process known as "quenching" as it was cast. This was a unique method in that most types of strengthened steel were made so by virtue of their chemistry. Certain additives make steel very strong, or very pliable or very dent resistant, etc depending on the application. But this method was a process solution that created this springy type of steel. The traditional method of making clips and clamps and widgets where a spring effect is required is to stamp it out of metal and then put the part through a secondary process called "heat treating" to give it the spring effect. (An example of a spring clip would be the tool rack in your garage that the handle of a broom or shovel snaps in an out of, with simply the pressure of the clip holding the handle). This new steel was springy in its raw state right from the mill. This allowed the metal stamper to create the part in one step, and also eliminate a second process altogether. So it was a very popular product.

After several years of a highly successful market rollout, the product was being used extensively in many different industries. The steel mill was riding high on their patented product, until one day, they got a customer complaint. Their customer complained that the usually very smooth, flat product was arriving with a "dimpled" appearance. The mill's initial response was to refer to the product specification which states a "no flatness tolerance or criteria". This was originally included in the product specs, because it was known that the product was subject to "coil set" which was this very stiff material tending to retain a bowed shape as it was unreeled from its packaging as a rolled up coil. The customer argued, "No, no, no, not coil set. This is tiny little golf ball sized dents throughout which appear on my finished parts. And that's not acceptable." The mill continued to push back through several months, and now hundreds of customer complaints, all with the same story. Some of the customers, dissatisfied and frustrated with the mill's unwillingness to recognize the problem, went back to the traditional method of stamping and heat treating their parts. They said it was the only way to ensure the quality of their products.

Loud enough were the shouts of the customers, eventually, that the mill gave in and agreed. The appearance had changed. They reluctantly agreed to reroll each and every produced coil to try to flatten it out as much as possible. There was a huge recall of all steel in the field. As the product was already hardened and stiff, it didn't respond well to this treatment, and customers remained frustrated.

Finally, a large enough customer complained and was considering removing the product from their purchased materials list. At this point, a problem solving team was put together by the mill. It was quickly discovered that as the material is cast and cooled, it was put through a water curtain to "quench" or freeze the material to make it stiff. The water curtain consisted of a line of small water spray nozzles. Because the original tank had been built out of plain steel, rather than stainless steel, there was rust inside the tank. The rust fines had gotten into the nozzles and clogged several of them. As the material was run through the water curtain, some areas were being sprayed, or quenched, and some

91

were not. This created puckers which really did look like dents created by golf balls. The tank was replaced, and the nozzles cleaned, and the product resumed its original high quality, smooth, flat appearance.

The great news is that the mill did eventually solve the problem. But not before it lost a great deal of goodwill among customers who also bought several other types of steel from them. And the users who had stopped using the product did not return. So it's important to create a business environment where the team members are willing to address a problem head on rather than resist or try to hide it.

Once you have defined the problem, get input from the subject matter experts. Identify as many root causes as you can. Then prioritize them based on which ones are the major contributors to the problem. Then, evaluate how complex solving each of them will be and tackle them one by one. Assign responsibility and a timeline – I call this, "Who and By When?". Assign a "Who and By When" to each of the solutions and have the team hold each other accountable for meeting the timeline. This is also critical to a successful corrective & preventive action system.

Root causes are elusive little creatures. They often travel in groups, but we rarely catch more than one at a time. When you are problem solving, and you identify a cause, don't stop there. Continue to brainstorm. First, use 5Y to ensure the root cause you've identified is the real root cause. And next, continue to ask yourself if there are additional root causes.

Once the solutions are in place, be sure to *verify* that the solution fixed the problem. This requires not only verifying that the prescribed action was taken, but also *validating* that it worked. Too often, the emphasis is placed on completing the action items in a corrective action. We put the issue to bed and call it closed because we did all the action items. Only to have the problem happen again, because we didn't actually get to the real root cause, or the solution we thought would work, didn't. Use the original data you gathered at the problem definition phase, and prove with the same data that the problem is solved.

Solutions are often changes to a process, so it is very important to continue to monitor the process to ensure the changes "stick". Many a problem has been solved over and over, because a solution or new method is identified, only to be dropped a few weeks later. When the new method is dropped, the problem comes back. This is called "snap back", because change is hard. And eventually, we snap back to our old ways. Having a solid and robust training process is the best way to ensure changes are implemented properly, and are not abandoned after several weeks. This is an example of how everyone must participate in the quality process, not just the quality team.

When the problem is solved, be sure to include a time period of surveillance to ensure, first that changes are permanent. And second, that the problem has actually been solved. Communicate regularly with the team. And be very visible to your organization when a corrective action is successful. Congratulate the team, and be sure to explain to everyone what the problem was and how it was solved. This creates that environment of trust and teamwork, but also provides clear examples of effective problem solving that everyone can learn from.

Finally, look for ways to capitalize on your success. Can you parlay this solution into preventive actions elsewhere? Take action right away in other areas which might be vulnerable to the same problem. If the solution could be applicable in other areas, and could help prevent a problem before it happens, get right on that and nip it before it causes you any more trouble!

EMBRACE PERFORMANCE REVIEW

So far, we've discussed how to set up an OES, and some high powered tools to get it moving forward. The best way to keep it moving forward, and to get results is through the use of an effective performance review.

Performance review, or a review of metrics is important for the continuing effectiveness of your system. The whole point of having a system at all is to improve the performance of the organization. And of course, to know whether you've improved or not, you have to have a way of measuring success.

We spoke at the beginning about defining the main processes of the organization, and then identifying a metric for each. Having done that, now we need to create a method of communicating our progress. The review of these metrics should be frequent enough to keep everyone informed, and the format should make the experience worth the time spent doing it.

Gather your management team, and agree upon a frequency of review. I prefer a monthly review for the first year or two of a new quality system. This is to vet out the metrics, establish a rhythm, confirm progress and manage resources. The metrics originally chosen for each process may need further thought or development. Or additional metrics may be needed. This will become evident as your monthly reviews continue.

Create a format. Will this be a formal meeting? A lunch meeting? An afterhours business meeting? Who should attend? Who *must* attend? Which metrics will be reported, and by whom? It is important for everyone to participate in the process. I prefer to have each department head report on his/her department's metrics. And I like the metrics to include productivity, safety, environmental and quality, with the department head taking ownership for all. Many times, companies have the safety manager report on safety. Who does that then suggest that safety belongs to?

When the format has been chosen, I like to use a template. This creates structure and clear expectations. If you and your management team decide on exactly what information should be included in each meeting, it will be covered and everyone will get the information they expect. I've learned from experience that leaving individual managers with creative license to report whatever they want, tends to neglect problems that need solutions, and resources that need to be requested and provided. Provide each manager with a template to create a brief summary of the metrics and goings on in their area. This should include information such as productivity, safety, environmental or regulatory compliance, 5S, corrective & preventive action, internal audit results, continual improvement initiatives and resource needs. This creates a balance of successes and challenges for the manager to present. This will ensure the management team gets a well-balanced summary of each department and their needs. This information should flow up to the business plan, and strategic decisions should include information from this monthly review.

Gather the group for a full review. It is essential that the top management attend the review, as it is mainly intended to inform them of status and needs so that they can take appropriate action going forward. But it is also beneficial for others, from various levels of the organization to attend, either regularly or on a rotating basis. Each manager's presentation should be brief, 5 to 10 minutes, and the time limit should be kept to less than 90 minutes, (with one hour being ideal). This requires a lot of preparation and discipline, but it makes for a powerful hour. People find the investment worth it when the information presented is relevant, and their time is respected. At the conclusion of the meeting, I also encourage managers to take their section of the review back to their departments to communicate to their team the same information that was presented to top management. This may include all, or a paraphrased version of the review as appropriate. Doing so creates a consistent message throughout the organization about the performance and action items in place to address the company's issues and needs.

A formal performance review is so important to keep your entire system on track. Using a template, you'll include a constant awareness of the key components of your business – productivity, safety, regulatory compliance, corrective & preventive actions, internal audits, continual improvement and the management of your resources to ensure the highest level of value and return on your investment.

IN THE FIELD

One of my most effective uses of the template approach was at a company with multiple locations. When I first started working with the company, the senior executives were frustrated. Because some of them were in charge of several locations, and corporate policy dictated that they attend the management reviews at each of them. They reported that some locations' reviews were very informative. They said they didn't mind going to them, because they found themselves to be very well informed after doing so. In other cases, they said the reviews were near torture. Their complaints ranged from the meeting lasting for hours with seemingly no structure, to the information being reported to actually being inaccurate.

I decided to use the template approach I had had success with in the past. This accomplished several things. As the company maintained certification to ISO9001, it was a requirement any way. But, we made sure that each location would review the same things the same way. And we were able to incorporate the required inputs and outputs as described in ISO9001. The template also helped the managers with their monthly assignment of reporting on their metrics. Some managers really struggled month after month to put something together. This helped tremendously. And finally, we were able to consolidate the reviews for several locations by creating a Quality Council. We were able to meet monthly via video conference and save some of those senior executives a significant amount of travel time. We really did take the opportunity to "lean up" the performance review process. And our audit results improved significantly.

HAVE EFFECTIVE MEETINGS

Meetings are definitely one of life's "necessary evils". And they are an excellent target for applying lean thinking. Meetings can really drain your company's time and resources if not manage properly. So much so, that I recommend that companies identify at least a general process for managing meetings and provide training to their entire staff, on a repeating basis, to the company's policy process for hosting meetings. Gather some of your biggest complaints, and distill them into something useful. Your company should always recognize meetings as potential source of waste, and should always look for ways to reduce that waste.

One very simple criteria I've heard is that everyone attending a meeting should have either provided information that no one else could, or should have received at least one action item. There are exceptions to this, of course, but it's a good general rule.

Hosting a meeting is a learned skill, and it takes practice to be a very effective meeting host. It's important to provide training and reinforcement to ensure that meeting effectiveness becomes an important part of your company's culture.

IN THE FIELD

In a true show of lean thinking, a former colleague of mine, we'll call him Joe, brought a very simple tool to an organization I worked with. He was an operations guy, but he really did embrace the concepts of quality and production working in synergy. He liked the idea of having a quality management system, while keeping it lean. And he ran the business with a multi-functional team, understanding that all aspects of the business – quality, productivity, environmental and safety must meet their goals for the organization to be successful. But he was not a big fan of meetings. Like many of us, he had little patience with sitting in meetings "noodling" ideas around the table. He also detested email as a means of requesting tasks and following up again and again and again. He was more of an action-oriented manager with a "Let's-just-get-it-done" attitude.

He brought what he called an "Accountability Board". I don't love the term, but the idea was to capture all those little action items that often get discussed in meetings and in hallways, but are left under the conference table as everyone walks out for their next cup of coffee. It was a tool to be used by the management team to ask for action from one another, negotiate a reasonable due date, and hold the responsible party accountable to meet the agreement.

It was a very simple, extra large dry erase board with a large grid. Across the top were the days of the month. Along the left edge, top to bottom, was a list of everyone's name on the team. The grid squares were exactly the size of a medium Post-It® or "sticky" note. When a task was required, the issuer would write their name at the top and a brief description of the requested task. Then they would write the responsible person's name at the bottom and put the sticky note in a parking lot area on the board. Each day, there was a brief stand up meeting where these tasks would be negotiated by the issuer and the responsible party. A date would be agreed upon, and the sticky placed in the appropriate slot in the grid. Each day, the previous day's "stickies" were reviewed and either given a green or red dot to indicate the agreement had been met. Red dots are, of course, taboo – especially in a public forum of your peers. This technique brought the team together and really helped get a lot of little tasks over the line. The team started working together more, and more got accomplished, because they learned to trust and rely on each other to get things done.

I've seen ideas similar to Joe's, but this one in its simplicity, was the most effective.

TOP 10 TOOLS

As we've moved through this review of some standard tools with a lean spin, let's review the main tools that can provide the highest yield in terms of establishing a robust business management system.

-The International ISO standards – they are a great place to start. Or explore the Malcolm Baldridge Award criteria, or pattern your management system after your major customer(s). But be sure to take their guidelines and customize them to make them work for your organization!

-A solid document control process – it is critical to ensuring that only the most accurate information is available for use. Be sure to keep the system easily accessible to users, though, or you may risk losing the effectiveness of this element of your system.

-A simple to use change management process – this is a great complement to your document control process, because as changes are made, the changes must be rolled out properly. Critical to making a change for the better, is that *everyone* make the change together. Be sure this process is created with effective implementation of change as its highest goal.

-A customer centric focus – lean thinking dictates that anything the customer isn't willing to pay for is waster – keep this in mind as you design *any* business management system.

-A process oriented approach – take time to understand what this means, and put it in practice *before* you get started to ensure the best chance at success. Knock down those silos so your team can work together to solve problems and find best practices.

-"8 week boot camps" – this is a very disciplined approach, with defined action items and timelines to define the details of your key processes and to provide a customized review of each process. This activity is very customer centric in that the area manager becomes the owner and the process parameters are created to his/her specification. This is a great tool to engage managers across your company in the creation and establishment of a comprehensive business management system.

-An extensive and effective internal audit process – it takes practice to make a habit. As new best methods are identified and continual improvement opportunities are discovered, an ongoing oversight to ensure changes are implemented and become permanent is imperative. The biggest challenge about creating an effective internal audit process is overcoming the stigma, and being consistent.

-A strong corrective & preventive action process using lean and Six Sigma – lean and Six Sigma are the best complement to effective problem solving. And effective problem solving is critical to the ongoing continual improvement of your business. Your organization must become comfortable and adept at bubbling up problems and solving them through a disciplined process of your own design using the many lean and Six Sigma tools available.

-A comprehensive and clear communication and performance review strategy – your team must be on the same page and heading in the same direction for your organization to achieve maximum success. Design and create a performance oriented company with goals and objectives, and measure (and celebrate) success regularly. Use this information to create a clear and consistent message so that every member has a sense of purpose each day. Let everyone have a sense of "I know where we're going, and I know what I have to do to help us get there".

-An effective meeting management process – improve your quality of life by making your meetings interesting and productive for everyone. Meetings are not fun for anyone, but if you put some effort into creating a company culture to value and preserve the investment of time put into meetings, everyone's life will be just a little bit more pleasant.

In all the years I've been lucky enough to work in the field of quality management and, quality-operations-environmental-safety-business management, I've discovered some masterful incorporation of old quality principles and new quality theories. And I've been inspired by the many quality enthusiasts I've worked with in an array of interesting industries.

These tools have time and time again, shown to yield the highest benefits. When sufficient time is put into their design and consistent use, they do wonders to establish your system. They quickly gain favor with the entire team, because they are concepts and tools that apply easily to almost any type of process. And they are sensible in that they are easily understood and easy to use.

Remember, the key to overcoming resistance and getting everyone in your organization to join your quality crusade is to make the system "invisible", meaning they don't even realize they're using it or "irresistible", so easy even a you-know-who could do it!

Now get out there and keep improving!

ONE LAST THING

When you finish this book please rate this book and share your thoughts on Facebook and Twitter. If you believe the book is worth sharing, please would you take a few seconds to let your friends know about it? If it turns out to make a difference in their lives, they'll be forever grateful to you, as will I.

I hope some of the insights and anecdotes I've provided help inspire you to think of your management system in new ways. Perhaps you think of a new way to leverage an old tool? Or perhaps you think of a component of your system in a new way with your own ingenious lean solution to a long nagging problem. I also invite you to share your feedback and your own stories with me on LinkedIn – http://www.linkedin.com/pub/marnie-schmidt-ssbb-cqa/24/a56/463. Also, visit my website at www.marnieschmidt.com and if you are interested in contracting my services to support development of your quality systems, please contact me.

ABOUT THE AUTHOR

Marnie Schmidt has a bachelor degree in Business Management, as well as Lean Six Sigma Black Belt certification and ASQ (American Society for Quality) professional certifications – Certified Quality Manager, Certified Quality Auditor and Certified Quality Technician with over 20 years of broad-spectrum, hands-on experience in management, sales & marketing, strategic planning, consulting, training and quality process improvement. She currently uses this experience as a freelance management consultant to help management teams create high powered business systems. She helps companies develop new systems, integrating quality, environmental and safety as well as improving traditional "ISO" quality systems by incorporating lean and Six Sigma to reduce waste and variation using a fast and repeatable management system implementation model that can be done in as little as eight weeks.

Questions or comments? E-mail me at marnie@schmidtproducts.com. Website: www.marnieschmidt.com
LinkedIn: http://www.linkedin.com/pub/marnie-schmidt-ssbb-cqa/24/a56/463

Made in the USA
Middletown, DE
11 March 2016